Be A Boxer
(Not a Fencer)

Be A Boxer
(Not a Fencer)

A Compendium of Notes Compiled by a
Philosophical Military Dude

Jason M. Dougherty

For FJ & Iris

Be A Boxer (Not a Fencer): A Compendium of Notes
Compiled by a Philosophical Military Dude

By Jason M. Dougherty

Copyright © 2024 Jason M. Daughterty

ISBN 978-1956-904-222

Printed in the United States of America

Published by Blacksmith LLC
Fayetteville, North Carolina

www.BlacksmithPublishing.com

Direct inquiries and/or orders to the above web address.

This book does not contain classified or sensitive information restricted from public release. The views presented in this publication are those of the author and do not necessarily represent the Department of Defense or its components.

While every precaution has been taken to ensure the reliability and accuracy of all data and contents, neither the author nor the publisher assumes any responsibility for the use or misuse of information contained in this book.

Acknowledgments

Thanks to everyone who has continually encouraged me over many years to write *something*. I doubt this is what anyone expected, me included, but I owe to each of you a substantial portion of my belief that I could do it. As the subtitle suggests, this book is an arrangement of notes that I've collected over the years. I've held many jobs, lived in many places, traveled the world, served in the military, and read a lot of books. I am a copious note-taker. Moreover, I have adopted the ideas of others and used my life and body as a laboratory.

Much of my seeking and experimentation have been to assuage a gnawing sense that there must be more than *this*, or simply to admonish myself to suck less when I was mismanaging myself. I've needed more help than your average dude. I distilled what I've collected into one place to clarify my thinking and to prepare myself to answer notional but profound questions, something along the lines of what our purpose in life is or what is the best way to live it. Were either of my children to ask me a question like that, I now have something to give them.

Any wisdom contained herein is not my own. These are the resources that have helped me along the way. I did my best to capture here some of the most important lessons and methods, the few I've been able to learn. I hope that I might offer someone a head start, or help a reader avoid a few of the mistakes that I've made.

I do not produce original thoughts. At best, I interpret and articulate in a way that points the reader toward the

Source. At worst, I misunderstand and misrepresent. I am deeply obliged to the men and women of my lifetime and history whose wisdom I briefly borrow, those shreds of it I comprehend. You've made my life better. In particular, the bedrock of my philosophy is built on the Stoics' simple and practical application methods and philosopher Dallas Willard's body of work, which explains realities in a way that I can (usually) understand.

Additionally, I owe my formation to the countless friends, family, and mentors who have influenced the way I see the world and have helped me when I could not help myself. Left to my own devices, I have a historical tendency to either overcomplicate or make an abject mess of things, particularly when they seem to be going too well. I have required leaders, mentors, and true friends to correct my course, again and again. I've been given many more second and third chances than I deserve. To them, I am forever indebted and profoundly grateful.

I am a fleeting steward of what I can hold, which is minimal. Life teaches profound lessons but I understand the lesson's meaning only through the "wisdom of the ages." As such, my words are plagiary of a noble kind. They amount to what others have taught me, that I have practiced, and I gratefully share to the extent that I can. Any failure to appropriately reference a source author or thinker is mine alone, so I abdicate all personal credit for the wisdom herein at the outset. The most sublime wisdom cannot be spoken. The rest we stumble through together. "This is not a long pull." (Stockdale)

Acknowledgments

"This is the true joy in life; the being used for a purpose recognized by yourself as a mighty one; the being thoroughly worn out before you are thrown on the scrap heap; the being a force of Nature instead of a feverish, selfish little clod of ailments and grievances complaining that life will not devote itself to making you happy."

"I am of the opinion that my life belongs to the community, and as long as I live, it is my privilege to do for it whatever I can. I want to be thoroughly used up when I die, for the harder I work, the more I live. Life is no 'brief candle' to me. It is a sort of splendid torch which I have got hold of for a moment, and I want to make it burn as brightly as possible before handing it on to the future generations."

– George Bernard Shaw

Contents

Introduction

"I believe that this experience of freedom to choose is one of the deepest elements underlying change . . . It is the burden of being responsible for the self who chooses to be. It is the recognition of a person that he is an emerging process, not a static end product."
– Carl A. Rogers, 1964

A fencer devotes years of her life to the mastery of the sword. Through grueling training and expert coaching, she wields her sword lethally, with elegant precision. She becomes one with the sword. The boxer undergoes similar training, subjecting himself to conditioning, strength training, and blows to the face. The boxer willingly subjects himself to beatings. The bludgeoning offers the lessons he must learn. He learns his lessons the hard way. The difference between them is that the fencer picks up her weapon to fight. When the fight is over, she lays it down again. Without her sword, the fencer is not dangerous. The boxer's weapons reside within him. At any time and in any scenario, the boxer is dangerous. His years of training shape him and he becomes lethal in body and mind, which act as one. The boxer *is* the weapon.

This is not a book about martial arts. The analogy of the boxer and the fencer was used by Marcus Aurelius to depict the path toward virtue. Gaining knowledge is essential, but putting knowledge into action requires that we know it by heart, for it is our hearts from which our words and actions spring, the place from which we *have our being*.

Introduction

I have never met an adult who does not feel that they could improve at least one area of their life. Energy is characterized as *potential* or *kinetic*. Potential energy is stored and unaffected by the external environment. Kinetic energy is particles in motion. When I think of a person (or of the world as an inexplicable wonder), I think of them in this way. They are both what I can observe and are orders of magnitude more. The complexity of a human being is unfathomable. Mental frameworks and bodily structures work interpretively to make sense of ourselves and each other.

Our systems provide a sense of place and relational identity, but we know we are much more. When I observe my children as they mature, I recognize within myself a response to their *potential*, a deep sense of the extent to which they are *unrealized*. When I met my spouse, I began to love her for the way she *was* but simultaneously was inspired by the way that she *could be*. Humans recognize in one another a depth of potential that speaks to us of our own. A part of us, unknown and unrealized, calls to that same part of another person. Deep calls unto deep. The deep part(s) of us that signify our potential recognizes the same part(s) in others. We *are* and we *are not yet*.

People want things. The human world is organized around desire. We often desire what is not in our best interest, what is not good for us, and ignorantly desire what we are constitutionally incapable of handling and haven't earned. I may want to be a high-paid CEO, but I don't know enough, I might not be smart enough, I'm inexperienced, and I don't want to work 80 hours per week. I may want my wife to have a sunny disposition and keep her figure, but year after year I get grouchier and fatter. I may want everyone to "do their job", but I can easily justify hiding and sliding while on the clock. I inhabit a delusional reality in which I enjoy the benefits of a well-lived life but am not required to pay the necessary price. I think that I'm a special case. I behave as if my rules for you don't apply to me. In such delusion, I'm owed things that I haven't earned and feel *inherently* deserving of privileges or special treatment; I'm *entitled*, a word that older folks enjoy using to describe young people.

The applications of *justice* and *fairness* demarcate an important distinction in this regard. When I fail to bring unconscious forces into my consciousness and call it Fate (Carl Jung), I let myself off the hook. Enough is enough. When I hold myself to a lower standard than I do other people, I have it backward. My life and the people in it reflect what I am. I attract in kind. Achievement is a combination of luck and discipline. The dictionary is the only place where "success" comes before "work", and there's no accounting for luck. It is all "on me." I must assume full responsibility for myself or shut my mouth. Better yet, I assume responsibility *and* shut my mouth. I am responsible for embodying my best. I may not require of others what I do not require of myself. My conduct matters and my opinions of others are best left unspoken.

There exists a well-known adage that an individual can create his or her own luck, e.g., *the harder I work the luckier I get.* This is true. Seneca is said to have proposed that "luck is when preparation meets opportunity."

Introduction

Digging further into antiquity, the Chinese character for luck is purportedly a combination of the two characters for *preparation* and *opportunity* or a similar combination. I have that on good authority, though I do not know Chinese nor did my research satisfactorily confirm it. Regardless, the concept is not a new one. I agree that disciplined and consistent preparation with an eye toward opportunity (which people often miss and it passes them by), yields good fortune in unexpected ways. Conversely, when a *chance* presents itself to rise to a specific occasion but finds a person incapable, ill-equipped, or afraid, the result can feel awfully like bad luck.

However, beyond the heartening or bludgeoning of chance, I believe that there are moments in life that appear as unearned gifts, as a grace dispensed, or as favor extended to us neither because of nor despite our actions. For these, it is wise to be aware and grateful and unwise to give ourselves credit. Luck in this sense is not based on preparation, nor is it a reward for hard work. It's a freebie. For it, we can neither account for its source nor account for it as a planning factor on the road to reaching our potential. Focus on your education, self-discipline, and growth, prepare to seize opportunities, and let sheer luck and unearned graces come as they may.

I must ask myself if I am willing to pay the price to become the kind of person who naturally inhabits any reality I can envision. To earn anything of value, or to achieve greatness of any kind, I must be willing to sacrifice. I must order my life into a rhythm that perpetuates continual growth along intentional lines. I must become the type of person who naturally has "that" kind of life. *The first and vital step is self-denial.* I must form a habit of self-denial. Only from perpetually practiced self-denial and relentless conditioning is intentional transformation possible, whether of the mind, body, or character.

Through acculturation, we all are formed and conform. Our belief systems are populated with licenses, prohibitions, mores, codes, hard laws, and soft guidelines that become a manual for how to behave in the culture in which we live. It is a social contract to conform, over time, to a cultural prototype. A well-ordered society depends on tacit collective agreements. Necessarily, many aspects of an individual must be muted to consistently present a culturally acceptable persona. The process is a kind of *dis-integration* of my personality.

In adulthood, after I have properly conformed and am confronted with the unrealized aspects of my personality, I may wish or be compelled to embark on transformation in one or many areas. Transformation is moving from conformity to one ideal to conformity to another (Willard) and reintegration of my personality is a crucial component. The choice before me then is to what new source of organized power will I now conform?

Authors like Viktor Frankl and Aleksander Solzhenitsyn tackled the meaning of life and the power resident within a single human being from places of sublime suffering. I learned much from their genius and wisdom, as millions have. But ignorantly, I've thought that having an epic battle to fight was the only way to a life of meaning, that unless

Introduction

I'm fighting the demon hoards at Armageddon from the front line of the assault, there is little fulfillment to be found in the churn of mundane life. I was wrong about that and it has cost me. A human can derive meaning in any circumstance. There is a purpose to be found on the dusty back roads of living, in the job you currently have, in the body you inhabit, and with the family and community into which you were born.

If you desire to become a more complete, useful, and actualized human being and are willing to make ongoing sacrifices, there is a way. *Volenti via est*, or, *for the one who is willing, there is a way*. A way is better than no way. If you want the power to access a better version of yourself and a reality that is richer, better, and more meaningful, keep reading. If you want something for free, or if you are unwilling to let go of the idea that you are a victim of circumstance, you may wish to read something more affirming. We decide how much we are going to matter. Our actions determine if we do. We must be reborn and renewed. Not deciding is a decision. As the Stoics say, character is fate.

We all want to matter in some way. We want to count for something. It's worth the effort to become someone who matters in ways important to us. Everyone is unique, but we share human qualities. None of us are exempt, none are special cases. Philosophy, psychology, mythology, and religion all offer insights into what it means to be human and how to access the "good life."

Andrew Huberman, Associate Professor of Neurobiology at Stanford, says "In the quest for neurological change, behavior comes first, then thoughts, feelings, and perceptions. Behavior is the driver of systems. Your behavior shapes your brain. The more often you perform an action or behave a certain way, the more it gets physically wired into your brain. This amazing adaptive quality of your brain is known as neuroplasticity." Additionally, what we fill our minds with and continually think about matters. The content of our thoughts shapes our worldview and determines how we *react* or *respond* to life. Behavior changes neurology; our thoughts (intentional or otherwise) change our perception of reality.

Knowing this and taking appropriate and consistent action is how you *become.* It's how a boxer becomes a weapon.

This book offers a method by which you can take stock of your life, establish first principles from which to operate, implement frameworks to prioritize effort, and sketch a map of the next required actions toward the realization of a clear vision. Each of us will change over time. The vital question is whether we change intentionally (toward growth) or unintentionally (toward deterioration). Pain is the touchstone of growth. This book captures a coherent framework that I devised to intentionally grow through the five levels of commitment along parallel lines of effort. It draws from many sources.

The Five Levels of Commitment:

1. Self-awareness (Holding up the Mirror)
2. Willingness to Change (Deciding: Once and then 100,000 times)
3. Intense Focus (Disciplined Learning)
4. Commitment (Disciplined Doing)
5. Character (Being)

Philosophy seeks to answer some version of four primary questions: 1) What is reality? 2) What is a good life? 3) Who is a good person? and 4) What is keeping me from those things?[1]

In an ordinary life, how does a man or woman become the "weapon" of his or her choosing?

This book is dedicated to a disciplined approach to understanding, deciding, and acting. It's an invitation to become the man or woman of your potential. I hope that this book is uncategorizable (could one find in it the philosophy section of the library, psychology, a soldier's diary, self-help?) in the sense that a human being is uncategorizable. We use categorical descriptors or labels to reduce and simplify humans into neat buckets because the complexity of a single human being is too vast a complication with which to contend.

At best, categorical generalizations provide an *idea* of what someone *might* be like, but they fail to capture even a hint of the uniqueness experienced during a one-on-one

---

[1] D. Willard, *The Divine Conspiracy: Rediscovering Our Hidden Life in God* (San Fransisco: Harper, 1988).

encounter. Authenticity bristles against labels. You are acculturated and influenced by the family and society in which you mature, but you are inexplicable at depth. The manic and often turnabout grasp for identity prevalent in today's Western culture indicates a profound lack of rooting in who we each are and what we mean to each other. It demonstrates our compelling human need to *belong*. It is tragic to observe a young person willing to trade anything, including their dignity, to belong to an ill-chosen tribe. For most, any tribe is better than no tribe.

Through understanding and education, the path outlined herein is one of vision, discovery, action, and reconnection toward a firm grasp of who you are, who you want to become, and your unique contribution to the struggle we collectively share with our brothers and sisters. Above all, we must not lose ourselves in heady abstractions. John Steinbeck wrote somewhere that the first rule of life is living. We seek to know so that we may better live.

1

Self-Awareness: Hold Up the Mirror

Part One: Be The Boxer, Not the Fencer

The Goal: The primary aim is to *become* the type of person who naturally achieves the goals you've set.

The first step in change is self-awareness. If you are satisfied with yourself in every way, there is no need to cultivate an awareness of yourself. If you feel like you have room for improvement in one or more areas of your life, if *anything* could be better, self-awareness is vital. I have heard talk therapy described as someone holding up a mirror so that you can see yourself for the first time, or through new eyes, or an aspect of yourself that you have not seen.

You become aware of traits and *sub-* or *un*conscious forces in your life. There are many ways to bring awareness. Combining knowledge with self-observation is one way. You ask yourself why you behave in certain ways and seek satisfactory answers to those questions. Most of us can benefit simply by learning about human personalities, and our psyches, and by paying attention to ourselves.

Mentorship, partnership, or professional guidance are indispensable along any growth chain. However, disabuse yourself of the misconception that you require a network of support (or an emotional support animal) or continual encouragement to set a new trajectory and stick with it. You don't. Marcus Aurelius said, "Beautiful things of any kind are beautiful in themselves and sufficient to themselves. Praise is extraneous." The object of praise is unchanged by praise; the object of ridicule is unchanged by ridicule. There are many resources available and many like minds from whom you can derive inspiration, but you do not need a cheerleader. Your commitment is your own. Learning to self-soothe is not limited to the agency of babies. It is not your words that will garner self-respect and the respect of others, it is your actions. The fewer people who know the better.

Self-worship lies at the root of our dysfunction. The cure for self-worship is self-denial. Hence, self-denial is the catalyst for improved function and the foundation for the proper reordering of the self's elements. Self-denial or good deeds when done quietly, "secretly", without drawing attention to themselves, are replete with intrinsic rewards. Secrecy is a discipline of its own in that it subordinates the human longing for recognition, the approval of others, praise, "points," or social credit. Secrecy combined with self-denial delivers a double reward. This is worthy of careful consideration. Think about it. Do your work. Keep it to yourself. Conversely, secrecy around misdeeds and myriad forms of self-worship exacerbate negative effects. A boss once told me that the only thing worse than a crime is a cover-up. Secrecy is a powerful advocate for good and a destructive partner in wrongdoing.

The human body is a system of systems. Organizations are a system of systems, as are sports teams, the stock market, modern medicine, our homes, and the universe. Systems have vulnerabilities, redundancies, and glitches. Systems are designed to produce predictable, desired outcomes. A system produces an effect. Effects analysis provides insights into how well a system functions and if it is the correct system for the desired outcome. In a system of systems, undesired effects are often the result of a dysfunctional system misinforming or hindering other systems in its constellation.

A program focused on improving a system must consider second and third-order effects in the family of systems. The Chesterton's Fence principle warns against altering an element until you understand why it exists. Don't tear down a fence in the middle of a field until you know why the fence was built. Becoming a boxer in life requires a systematic systemic approach. It must be systematic to reduce complexity to manageable elements. It must be systemic to formulate accurate assessments of healthy function, with a focus on redesigning, taxing, or refueling a system to optimize the effect it produces with awareness of collateral effects on sister systems. Divide your vision until it's indivisible.

This enables specificity and precision when identifying causative factors. It may not be your "job" that frustrates you, but a single "system" within the totality of your job that yields unwanted results. "Poor health" can be the result of any number of specific variables or a combination of them. Acknowledging that I am unhealthy is too vague a thing to address. To act, I must eliminate variables and narrow my focus to take precise actions toward improvement. As in weightlifting, those are each a single repetition, within a set, within a session of sets, within a program. The objects we see are trillions of invisible things. The world is composed of atoms and quarks and maybe smaller elements than that; helicopters are built from thousands of parts and fly (usually) because those parts work together in unison; everything that we can do comprises unique parts, steps, actions, and thoughts. Our synapses fire first this way and then that, millions of snaps, an electrical storm in our bodies, constellations of lightning strikes.

Additionally, compartmentalizing human systems and functions as autonomous, or disconnected from all other functions, is not only untrue but also the source of internal conflicts, confusion, and a tendency to divide ourselves into parts rather than appreciate our wholeness. "The American spiritual genius Jonathan Edwards ... steadfastly opposed all efforts 'to divide human nature into separate compartments of mind, will, and emotion.'" "We may be distinguishable, but we are not divisible. To be "mixed" is not to be divided; a stew is not a salad bar."[1] (The "natural" war between the head and the heart is fictional.

---

[1] E. Kurtz and K. Ketcham, *The Spirituality of Imperfection: Storytelling and The Search For Meaning* (New York: Bantum, 1992), 73.

The head requires that the heart quicken it and the heart that the head temper it. They are designed to be siblings, not combatants. The connectedness of our parts and our connectedness to others is "perhaps, the most important human experience. It is certainly the deepest human desire."[2] The authors focus on an "essential spiritual truth: the importance of avoiding the dichotomizing, diving-into-two approach that is the bane of all spirituality."[3]

Re-membering puts pieces back together. The word *religion* means to *bind again*, to reassemble into wholeness. The theme of spirituality spans well beyond orthodoxy and traditions. It captures the essence of what it means to be human. The family of systems inherent to each human being is comprised of the heart, mind, body, social context, and soul.

> *Heart*: volition, will, and spirit. The heart can "*originate* things and events that would otherwise not occur. Involving both freedom and creativity, the *power to originate is the power to do what is good or evil*."[4]

> *Mind*: interdependent thoughts and feelings that are mutually corresponding. Thoughts do not occur without feelings nor do feelings occur without

---

[2] Ibid., 72.
[3] Ibid., 38.
[4] D. Willard and D. Simpson, *Revolution of Character: Discovering Christ's Pattern for Spiritual Transformation* (New York: NavPress: 2005), 28.

thoughts. Though distinct, they are included in what we label our minds.[5]

Body: "Our personal presence in the physical and social world." The body is our primary source of energy and strength and has a tacit knowledge of its own. Training the body results in 'discipline without discipline', discussed later, wherein habit resides, within our body, which acts without requiring thought.[6]

Social Context: humans require other humans and humans require a Higher Purpose. Our social context encompasses human relations as well as our relationship with God or a Higher Power.[7]

Soul: "The soul is that dimension of the person that connects all of the other dimensions so that they form one life."[8]

If I employ a well-worn method of introspection by imagining myself on my deathbed, I do not envision a man listing his accomplishments to his bedside vigil. Recently, I explored a nearby graveyard with headstones up to 200 years old. A surprisingly small number of them had thoughtful epitaphs. How does one distill an entire life into a single sentence? I think I've probably heard 15 or more

---

[5] Ibid., 27.
[6] Ibid., 30-31.
[7] Ibid.
[8] Ibid., 32-34.

pastors and motivational speakers use this device. I didn't devote any time to considering what mine might say.

Despite my best efforts, a question materialized in my mind, "What do I want to have been known as?" This feels like a rewording of the question, "How do I want to be remembered", but they are not the same. *Remembered as* and *known as* are distinct. The least reliable evidence in a court of law is an eyewitness. Memory is suspect, particularly when it comes to family. Even the worst mother is often remembered as some version of a woman who meant well, persevered through personal struggles, or did the best she could. Memories gild truth to insulate pain.

To be known is to be experienced. It requires human exchange. It requires a sharing of physical space, words, energy, and spirit. It's at the center of the idea that people rarely remember what I say but they always remember how I make them feel. *"To be known as"* requires that I align any goals I set with a path meandering toward that version of myself. I must know how that version of me thinks and acts, what his guiding principles are, and how he makes the people around him feel.

From a *clear vision* of that man, I can begin to disassemble my life to identify inferior functions. Breaking it down enables you to simplify the long journey to *becoming that person* into single steps on your chosen path. Understanding where your path leads is vital to this process. I need little to begin. Like the early settlers of the United States, told to "go west", I need only a direction. As

I travel, each step will reveal the next. If my cardinal direction remains true, the deviations and detours of life are of no lasting consequence.

With a clear vision, all paths lead to the Center. I am free to focus on each step, to enjoy it as I take it, and to rest easy knowing that I will be ready for the next step when the time comes. The *path* is not my life, but simply its trajectory. The *steps* are my life in the poetic sense of an entity in motion. Our lives are lived through our bodies. Memorable moments are rare and fleeting. My life is the thousands of small steps that I take.

My life is found in the routine and the mundane. *The quality of my life is determined by what I think and do repeatedly, all day, every day.* My life is how my spouse looks at me when I walk in the door at the end of the day. The trajectory of the path determines which steps I choose to continue taking, what to start, and what to stop. I am free to deliberately take and more fully experience each step on its terms.

Being a boxer is the alchemy of turning ideas into material substance. It is the tactical expression of strategic imperative or the conversion of guiding principles into tangible actions, the stuff of life. Integrity is the alignment of what I say and what I do. When my thoughts, perceptions, and actions are aligned, and the functional energies of each facet of my personality are activated, I am integrated. I become whole. Through character comes consistency, the decompartmental-ization of the self so that I am the same in any context. I can be relieved of the duplicitousness of acting one way at home, another at work, and another when hanging out with the lads.

We can honestly be who we are. One philosophical angle is phenomenology, which asserts that our bodies are primary in the gaining of knowledge. Rather than merely an academic pursuit, it is an experiential one. Observation reveals the truth. Experience is comprised of the harmony or cacophony of mind, body, and spirit acting as a system of systems. It is also an experimental one. Each mind-body-spirit system of systems responds in unique ways to different experiences. You are your own test case.

Philosophy 101-The Deliberate Life: "There is a limit to the time assigned to you. If you don't use it to free yourself it will be gone and never return...Do everything as if it were the last thing you were doing in your life, and stop being aimless, stop letting your emotions override what your mind tells you, stop being hypocritical, self-centered, and irritable. You see how few things you must do to live a satisfying and reverent life...Everyone gets one life. Yours is almost used up. Instead of treating yourself with respect, you have entrusted your own happiness to the souls of others"[9]

A philosophical outlook prepares a person to contend with calamity, fear, and reversals of fortune. A philosophical outlook is also a historical outlook. U.S.

---

[9] Marcus Aurelius, *Meditations*, 14.

Marine General Jim Mattis said that history provides "old solutions to new problems." History teaches us about how people have dealt with failure and success, and how, contrary to human desire, virtue is not always rewarded nor evil punished. Bad things happen to good people. Rain falls on the just and the unjust. Things don't always work out. The formal military decision-making process includes *wargaming*.

Proposed courses of action are introduced to a "Red Cell", a team often comprised of intelligence personnel, who play the part of the enemy in combat. It is an exercise of "move" and "countermove" to identify weaknesses in the plan and provoke contingency planning not for *if* the plan is disrupted, but *when*. Cultivating a philosophical outlook requires intentional forethought and preparation to meet with courage, emotional stability, and functional utility the variables that life presents, from inconveniences to catastrophes.

Philosophy seeks to answer *first-order* questions. In two broad categories, philosophy can be either *theoretical* or *normative*. Theoretical philosophy is primarily concerned with being or existence (metaphysics), with becoming (philosophy of nature), or with knowledge (epistemology). Normative philosophy concerns itself with the "good life", right and wrong, and conduct *appropriate* for a good human, i.e., what we *ought* to do. [10]

---

[10] *How to Read a Book*, 275-277.

A philosophical theology (based on my readings of Willard) presents the concept that there exist two concrete and observable realities, one seen directly and the other indirectly. The inferior of the two is that which can be seen directly, what we think of as "the world." It is a secondary reality.

This *secondary* reality is plainly observed at work in lives obsessed with money and things, with appearance and looking good, and in exerting control over others. In short, it is fueled by selfish willpower. What I fail to understand in pursuit of such a life is that while I seek to subject the world to my will, I inadvertently become a slave to my will.

A life fueled by self-will is ultimately self-defeating. My will demands, and I obey. The superior of the two realities is the one that we can only observe indirectly. It is the *primary* reality, that which is organized around first principles, often encapsulated as *The Logos*. The primary reality is accessible indirectly through disciplined subjection of my will to a Higher Will. *A life of self-denial is the repeated act of choosing a superior life over an inferior one.*

There is an inextricable link between Stoic philosophy and God. The preeminent Stoic philosopher Seneca, though a polytheistic pagan, experienced a preeminent Divinity and wrote in Letter 41 that "God is close to you, he is with you, he is within you. That's what I mean, Lucilla: a holy spirit lives within us, the one who notes our good and bad actions and is our guardian. As we treat this spirit, we are also treated by him. In fact, no man can be good without God's help." From Seneca's descriptions of discovering God in nature comes the idea of living according to Nature.

The Goal: A tree is known for the fruit it bears. The point of philosophical orthodoxy and orthopraxy is to get better and be better as a human being. My wife described it succinctly as a general pursuit to "Do good for God", capturing the essence of my part, my purpose, and my context. Such a pursuit can draw from either category of philosophy. The result is that you live a better life. You become more capable, resilient, productive, useful, and content.

My discovery has been primarily along the lines of conformance to natural law, the conduct of a good man, and how to *become* someone like that. Abe Lincoln said that whatever you decide to be, be a good one. I'm a human. I want to be a good one. The Stoics say that well-being depends on good luck or good character. Only one of those is within my power. I do what I can and worry less about what I cannot. I must also define for myself what character, virtue, and goodness mean to me, *precisely*. What is justice, honesty, discipline, courage, or humility? Why are those aspirations worthy of my time and attention? If for no other reason, the cultivation of character engenders *endurance*, the ability to hang tough under pressure.

The Stoic and Epicurean methods, different though they were, each sought to equip their disciples to make the best of a short life fraught with pain, evil, violence, and nastiness of all kinds. It is difficult after two millennia of global Judeo-Christian influence to fully grasp the utter despair that saturated human existence in pagan antiquity. In that world, the gods destroyed humans for sport, kings had unfettered authority to abuse or take human life, and all men were unequivocally not thought to be created equal.

Even the Stoics failed to solve the primary problem of evil in the world, aside from what Dallas Willard referred to as "soul management." Willard as a logician argues that the problem *was* finally solved and that Jesus of Nazareth, first as rabbi and consummately as Christ, framed the "how-to" guide for individual and societal reformation. Regardless of anyone's beliefs about Jesus as the Messiah, the fact of his revolutionary influence for the good of human history is irrefutable. Everything we know in the Western world of the "inalienable rights" of humans, particularly those disenfranchised, trodden upon, outcast, and subjected, emerged from the metaphysical and epistemological insurrection that he originated and initiated.

Henry Rollins, poet, punk rocker, and weightlifter said of his transformation in the gym that weights never lie. "200 pounds is always 200 pounds." I can fool myself, but I can never fool a loaded bar of weights. A loaded bar always gives me honest feedback. I must be willing to look in a mirror and contend with what I see. Dallas Willard wrote extensively on what it means to be a "good person" and how to become one. Willard insisted that we must *become* that to which we aspire.

An analogy Willard used was a man who wanted to pick up a significant amount of weight, say 500 pounds, from the ground. Physical fitness has been central to my program since I was a teenager. I've set many different types of fitness goals and strived to achieve them: run faster, get bigger, gain strength, or function better in specific environments. No amount of sheer willpower enables me to lift 500 pounds from the ground. I must become the kind of man who can naturally perform such a feat. To become that man, my life must be ordered or reordered in such a way that, over time, I slowly grow into that man. I must adhere consistently to a training program that enables incremental strength gains toward that end. I must eat enough nutritious food. I must rest and recover purposefully.

My mind must focus on the goal and eliminate distractions along the way. I become such a man slowly, intentionally, and one repetition at a time. If I stay the course long enough, I may one day step to the bar, take a deep breath, and pull 500 pounds from the ground. The change happens gradually. The power of "Before and After" photos captures the contrast. We don't remember what we looked like a year ago. A man capable of lifting 200 pounds is not the same type of man as one who can lift 500 pounds. The two men look, think, and carry themselves differently. The man who has traveled from 200 pounds to 500 pounds has reordered the rhythm of his life to ensure consistency in training. He has honed self-discipline to make sacrifices of time, in his diet and with competing activities. When given a choice whether to train or to (pick one) sleep, relax, go to the movies, or get drunk, the man chooses to train. He is mentally tougher. Hard training is tough. Sometimes it hurts. The man strains muscles, gets sore, and scrapes skin off his body.

There is blood. He continues to train. He continues to do the work. He persists. His mind discounts pain as a small price to pay for strength. After traveling this path for some time, the man is strong. He has become the kind of man who can naturally lift 500 pounds. Feats of strength flow from him because he has trained for them. To look at him or to know him, it makes sense that he is capable of such a feat. He mustn't *try* to look, act, or be strong, he simply *is*. Over time, the disciple of strength alters his core *identity*, a principle salient to lasting change of any kind. The training of the body, the mind, and character are of like kind.

In today's online world of avatars and photo filters, people present theatrical constructs of themselves. We can invent a glossy version of ourselves and blast that nonsense across the globe in an instant. It amounts to being doubly fraudulent, as the avatar is constructed from the egoic persona, which is itself a construct of the real person. Copies of copies get blurry. Citizens of the digital world have a tacit agreement to pretend it's real. It *is* a *kind* of reality, just as movies depict the screenwriter's take on a story. People pull off the impossible in movies. We willingly suspend our disbelief for entertainment.

After the movie, we walk into the cool embrace of the night air, toward the car we drive to work every day, under a canopy of stars. Back to our world. The danger of photo-shopped profiles and carefully crafted online stories is not in the pretending. Humanity has been doing versions of this forever. But I stare down the barrel of a gun when I confuse my avatar with myself or judge and belittle myself in comparison to it. I must not conflate my online character with the sovereign skin sack of bones and blood that requires care and feeding. It is hilariously disastrous when the stark contrast between a man's online digital dating ego and the dude who physically shows up for the first date results in public humiliation.

If you have time to squander, have fun online. Filter your pictures. Be the god of your myth. Everyone loves a good story. When the fun is over, remember it's not you. You have important work to do.

The Stoic philosophers, Marcus Aurelius among them, distinguished between types of mastery. They'd say, don't master the weapon, become the weapon. In philosophy, don't merely know what rational thought is, think rationally. Put into practice what you've learned. Embody it. Become a rational being. A fencer trains with her sword. She becomes an expert at wielding it. Over time, she develops the strategic mind of a warrior, the tactical skills of swordplay, and the body of an athlete. Elite-level fencers develop considerable power and endurance through strength training and conditioning in addition to their study of weaponry. She is dangerous ... *when she has her sword*. The boxer undergoes a similarly rigorous regimen and is honed into an equally dangerous foe. The difference between them is that the boxer's weapons reside within the boxer, they are organic to the boxer. The boxer *is* the weapon. A boxer fighting a fencer who has a sword has some chance of winning.

If the boxer can use footwork to get inside or gets lucky, the odds improve. A fencer who has no sword and fights a trained boxer gets a one-sided beat down. The analogy is not meant to disparage the sport of fencing but to illustrate the point. The same could as easily be said of a rifleman or corporate marauder as a fencer. A less martial analogy is a musician and a dancer. The musician creates art through an instrument, while the dancer's moving body is the art. The Stoic mindset is to advance from knowing that the proper use of available tools can make us better, to using them effectively, to becoming the type of person who embodies them. Know the weapon, use the weapon, become the weapon. Have – Do – Be.

Who do I want to *be*? How do I want *to be known*? Regardless of what my mother told me, I cannot do anything I set my mind to. I will never solve complex applied mathematical equations in my head. I will never be taller. I will never run a mile in less than four minutes. I will never have a different bloodline. Most likely, I will never have a billion dollars. If someone gave me a billion dollars, I would not know how to manage it. I am not the type of person capable of handling a fortune well. Most likely, it would destroy me. But I can learn patience. I can lose (or gain) a few pounds. I can be silent when I don't know what I'm talking about. I can give money or time to help others. I can get stronger. I can recognize that I'm the common variable in my string of failed relationships. I can think rationally about a situation and respond with clarity, humility, and grace. I can persevere.

Marcus Aurelius said that the only rewards of a life well-lived are unselfish actions and unstained character. *Who I want to be* is not a question of profession, possessions, or position. It is a question of character. Character is fate. *Your* character is *your* fate. I have choices about how I will relate to the life I live and the people who populate my life. I have my hands full learning how to be a good dude. If I focus on that, most other things take care of themselves.

The Why: Stronger bodies are more useful than weaker ones. A strength coach named Mark Rippetoe said "Stronger People are Harder to Kill and More Useful in General." In gritty garage gyms and warehouse weight rooms across the globe, rough men and women train unseen, devoted to function and utility. These hard characters care little about six-pack abs or bulging biceps, though they often have them. The point of lifting heavy things is so that I can lift heavy things. Hard things keep me from going soft. Physical training is a pathway of personal development with tangible tools and visible results. It's accessible to almost anyone. Minds housed in healthy bodies function better.

All systems in the human body are mutually supporting. When one system is optimized, all other systems improve. A strong body makes for better digestion, a clear mind, and deeper sleep, and it improves overall mood. Fitness provides a psychological edge. Continually subjecting yourself to the strain and pain of rigorous training puts other everyday challenges in their proper place. Doing hard things makes other things look easy. The development of physical fitness is one primary line of effort among several. The framework is transferrable.

In William A. Henry III's book *In Defense of Elitism*, he adeptly debunks egalitarianism as a worthwhile substitute for equality. The two are not the same. Equality requires that any individual has a spot on the starting line. Egalitarianism insists that everyone cross the finish line together. Not everyone deserves an equal outcome. We earn our outcomes predicated upon our efforts, our natural abilities, and our disciplined dedication toward self-improvement. Individuals who work harder deserve more than those who don't. Smarter people have a potentially easier time navigating life than dumber people, though smarts do not ensure success. Grit prevails more often than talent. We work with what we have. When I'm below average in one area, I must make up for it in another area where I have an advantage. If I use any lack of advantage as an excuse, I doom myself to perpetual failure.

If I desire to stand in the company of great men and women, I must lead the kind of life that makes me fit company. If you work harder and smarter longer than me, you're better than me. If I outsmart and out-hustle and out-work you, I'm better than you. We take this concept for granted in sports and in the military, where "elite" athletes and operators are heralded. They're accepted as being better than others. What is often missed is the gravity of the sacrifice required to be *that good* at something, the sheer amount of hard work done behind the scenes.

The best aren't born that way. You must invest heavily in a talent to actuate it. Among the unwashed masses, the idea of elitism is unacceptable through the lens of egalitarianism. Regardless of political narratives and social trends, elitism conforms to nature. The law will persist no matter how we feel about it. I can ask myself, "Who do I want to be?" Immediately thereafter, I must ask myself, "Am I willing to pay the price?"

Jim Wendler, a strong man, author, and honest coach, answered the question "Why Train?" Among his reasons were "To challenge yourself mentally and physically"; "To develop the bite that may help you through difficult times"; "In a world of 'easy' it keeps your teeth sharp"; "To understand that there is cause and effect to action and to inaction"; "Fat, weak, and ignorant is not a good role model"; "To exhaust your body and mind so as to put up with weak fools and ignorant beggars who demand what you have earned"; "To learn self-reliance"; and "Because a mentally and physically dangerous man will always be needed."[11]

Stronger minds are more useful than weaker ones. Rational minds beat irrational minds. Vice Admiral James Stockdale was a U.S. Navy fighter pilot who was shot down during Vietnam. A collection of his essays and speeches

---

[11] https://www.jimwendler.com/

introduced me to Stoicism. He spent seven years as a prisoner-of-war in the notorious "Hanoi Hilton", five of those years in solitary confinement. Before capture, Stockdale was earning a master's degree as part of his military education.

After finishing his required courses, he began auditing philosophy courses. He was introduced to Stoicism and to a philosopher named Epictetus. Epictetus was a Roman slave who earned his freedom through philosophy. As a slave, he had been beaten and tortured. As a philosopher, he still carried the limp and scars. Stockdale read with fascination Epictetus' view on life, that there are two universal categories: 1) what I can control, and 2) what I cannot control.

The list of those things that I control is short. The extent of my control ends at the boundary of my skin. Beyond my body and what resides within it, I have little to no control. As an example, I may exert influence over others' behavior, but I will never control it. Confusion about this leads to suffering. If my happiness depends on the behavior of another person, it amounts to premeditated disappointment. Irrational desire is an agreement with myself to be unhappy until I get the world to do what I want.

Seneca said that he would rather beg of himself not to desire a thing than beg the Fates to bestow it upon him. The roles that desire and aversion play in our lives are worth understanding and contemplating. The world is indifferent. Accepting this is the first step toward freedom.

We do not recognize the weight of the chains that bind us to our unfulfilled needs. Freedom is to become acutely aware of our limited capacity and a practiced, rational focus on what we can control. Simultaneously, I must learn to release that which I do not control into the capable hands of God. I must inhabit a place where simply put, I am, and it is. I have my hands full with myself. I focus on that and let the world spin without my judgment or the inevitable exhaustion from trying to manage it.

As prisoners of war, despite torture, starvation, disease, and humiliation, Stockdale said that it was not those conditions that ultimately killed Americans. Captured servicemen were trained to divulge no information to the enemy, except "Name/Rank/Serial Number." In the hands of a professional torturer, within minutes any man was willing to spill information to make it stop. No one could withstand it.

Returning to their cells, the guilt and shame of having failed to keep their oath were debilitating. Once they'd relinquished hope, they'd die of a broken heart. It broke their will to live. The chain of command remained in effect, even as prisoners. Stockdale was the senior officer. He rewrote the Code of Conduct to preserve the dignity of his fellow prisoners. To live well, or in dire circumstances to live at all, a person must be able to look in the mirror and feel self-respect. When I fail, I know it was not for lack of trying. Stockdale knew this from his study of Stoicism. He led his fellow inmates toward a community mindset, offering clear expectations and a mutually supporting code by which to survive.

He devised a covert method of communication so that they could stay connected and share the experience. Stockdale honored the code. When he was scheduled to appear in a propaganda video to corroborate the humane treatment of the prisoners, Stockdale bludgeoned his face with a three-legged stool so they couldn't put him on camera. As horrific as it was, Stockdale provided a primitive tribal arrangement where the prisoners were part of something bigger than themselves, where they could contribute to the common good, and where they could connect in mutual respect and love.

Many prisoners there attributed their survival to Stockdale's leadership. Like Epictetus, Stockdale carried a limp for the rest of his life, a result of injuries from repeated torture. For his actions, he was awarded the Congressional Medal of Honor. One Christmas day during his incarceration, locked in solitary confinement, Stockdale's fellow prisoners were mopping the floor outside his door. He noticed a rhythm to the mopping. In Morse Code, they spelled out over and over, "We love you."

The How: Curiosity is a barometer for psychological health. Self-smart yourself. Become an autodidact. General Mattis said, "If you haven't read 100s of books you're functionally illiterate. Personal experience alone is not enough to sustain you." Lifelong autodidacticism, when persistently pursued, creates in a person utility, adaptability, substance, depth, scope, and the ability to connect seemingly disparate elements (functional genius). It also makes you more interesting during dinner conversation. Learn something new. It's a log thrown on the fire of life. Failure is the point. Keep at it.

The Greek Stoics assert that an obstacle does not stand in the way of growth, *it is the way*. Epictetus said, "From everything which is or happens in the world, it is easy to praise Providence, if a man possesses these two qualities, the faculty of seeing what belongs and happens to all persons and things, and a grateful disposition. If he does not possess these two qualities, one man will not see the use of things … another will not be thankful for them, even if he does know them."[12]

Our faculties are given to us free from hindrance. Challenges are opportunities to recruit and employ our natural faculties so that we may become who we can become and are designed to be. We neither seek nor avoid such challenges but treat them as we would a weight to be lifted or a chore to be done so that we may become stronger or restore order. Epictetus challenges us to invite means by which we may be exercised. "Bring now, O Zeus, any difficulty that you please, for I have means given to me by you and powers for honoring myself through the things that happen." This picture provides a stark contrast with the cowering man who hides, malingers, or blames. "Yet I will show you that you have the powers and means for greatness of soul."[13]

Be Resourceful. The idle poor and the idle rich are similar. The primary difference is that the poor are much

---

[12] Epictetus, *Enchiridion*, 27.
[13] Ibid., 27-29.

more creative (and interesting). "Teaching oneself" does not mean that I do not learn from others. On the contrary, the autodidact seeks knowledge for him or herself from people, groups, books, personal experience, and the wonder of the internet. Systematize your learning. Dedicate structured time to learning new things at a time of day when there is never a conflict (e.g., 4 a.m.). Devote 60 minutes every morning. Read, meditate, draw, or learn a new skill. Memorize poems or scripture. Learn *something*. Then train. Walk, do push-ups, run, or go to the gym. Do all of this before the start of your workday.

When you step into your routine day, enjoy the feeling of having already gotten better. While everyone else was asleep, you got smarter and stronger. When I am dedicated to learning, I find that people are more interesting. I realize that everyone knows things that I don't. If I am open, I can learn something from someone every day. People will teach me what to do and what not to do.

Keep Your Sense of Humor. We're here for a good time, not for a long time! During a rough transition in my life, several major life events occurred in short order. I was divorced from an 18-year marriage, ended my military career, and moved across the country to start work in an industry in which I had never worked.

One month, I was a military commander, and a few months later I was flipping hamburgers in my brother and sister-in-law's restaurant, an entry-level position for which I was generously overpaid. I hadn't lived in the town I moved to for over 25 years. I had no friend group or network there. I rented a house. Six months later, I realized one day that none of my pictures were hung, I had an entire room full of unpacked boxes, and I had never plugged in my television. I had lost sense of who I was and had yet to determine who I wanted to be in the next chapter of my journey. I drank too much, had reckless romantic relationships, and generally approached life with a "whatever" attitude.

I had not leveraged military leadership experience for a lucrative civilian position and began a meteoric rise through C-suite ranks, optimizing for a sublime fusion of martial wisdom and cold-blooded capitalism, as many career military officers envision. I moved to an island and got drunk. It was not in an "I've earned this" kind of way, but more of a "What's the point" kind of way. I later learned that my life's purpose had failed to transcend my vocation, a dangerous mistake. I knew I needed to find solid ground and formulate a vision, but it was taking time. I used to joke, "Please be patient with me. I'm screwing things up as fast as I can!" In those moments, I didn't doubt the core of my being or discount previous successes, or more likely I did.

Regardless, I knew I wasn't living my best life, i.e., I wasn't tapped into expressing my potential, and I knew that would have to change. I was just getting by. Calling myself out brightened my outlook and reminded me that I had not yet given up. The whole underwhelming mess of my life was funny, even when I was the hapless protagonist in the story. It is important to note that pain and joy can coexist. Indeed, pain often amplifies joy in contrasts profound. Ironically, it was not until I finally "gave up on myself" that I broke through the morass. On the other side of that transition, many things have changed. Now, I screw things up more slowly.

Routinely, my mind makes living harder than it is, especially when I fail to notice how joy is woven into my very existence. Any day I live will be exactly how it will be. I must remind myself that I have a choice to enjoy it or endure it. When I downshift mental gears, I am reminded of how loaded with pleasure human life is. Every compulsion mandatory for the sustainment, functioning, and perpetuation of human life is enjoyable: breathing, sleeping, bathing in water, basking in sunlight, relieving ourselves in the bathroom, sex, the smells, taste, and texture of food, quenching thirst, burping, farting, and the sensation of touch. Why is the word "fart" never *not* funny? Even the wrenching discomfort of vomiting is rewarded with a deep sense of relief, often approaching euphoria. *Wow, I feel so much better!* Pleasure, and the joy we derive from it, are built in. Joy leads to laughter. Foibles are funny. Keep your wits – and your wittiness – about you.

Examine Your Beliefs. Regardless of what I swear, propose, intend, or "know", I will ultimately behave according to my beliefs. My aim in the study of and adherence to an ethical code, philosophy, or religion is not limited to learning about them, which is necessary, or how to think critically, which also is a valuable skill. I aim to decide for myself what is true to obtain moral certitude as a basis for how I choose to live. A simple illustration from my own life is that of professional medical advice. As a young man, I believed that doctors were properly educated and compassionately motivated to offer guidance regarding my physical health, including nutrition and exercise. I followed "doctor's orders."

As I became increasingly self-educated and experimented with nutrition and exercise in myriad ways, the results of my efforts sometimes stood at odds with the medical majority. One example is that multiple doctors told me that a diet where 40% of my calories were derived from good fat would result in high cholesterol, high blood pressure, and heart disease, all of which run in my family. Year after year, my medical physicals indicated the opposite. During a military post-deployment physical, a rotund and visibly unhealthy doctor, afflicted with shallow breathing, powder-pale skin blotched with pink and red archipelagos, and a light coat of perspiration, lectured me on the evils of lifting heavy weights and insisted that the bulk of my calories ought to come from simple starches and carbohydrates, presenting a circa 1980s food pyramid for my edification.

For the first time in my life, still edgy from eight months in a combat zone, I rebelliously retorted that the good doctor might give himself a physical and reconsider his stance on both matters, for either he was mistaken or he was ignoring his own advice. The proof is in the pudding, I said. With that, he stamped my form "fit for duty" and walked out of the exam room without saying a word. Whether right or wrong, I tailored my diet to what I *believed* about nutrition and avoided what I *disbelieved,* contrary to what I *knew* the medical establishment published.

Our parents and institutions instill our initial beliefs. As teens and adults, we are unconsciously motivated to behave according to beliefs about ourselves, i.e., what we were told about ourselves when we were young. Told we are smart, stupid, ugly, beautiful, slow, athletic, fat, amazing, funny, capable, or a POS ("You're just like your father"), these beliefs become drivers and limiters later. Beliefs about the world ("it's a dangerous place!") or about people (you can depend on the kindness of others; inherently "bad" or "good"; "you can't trust anybody") shape who we become. Beliefs and religion go together; many profess but do not exemplify. When a boss has a "good idea" but her team does not agree (believe), progress will be slow until there is consensus.

What is crucial to understand is that I may believe something that is *not* true and I may disbelieve something true. Knowledge is crucial to visiting my beliefs and altering them where appropriate. Knowledge can be gained through study or bodily action and tested results attest to certain truths. Such experiments can be invaluable in reshaping my self-image, my perspective on the world, or my beliefs about God. A belief that I am stupid may keep me from performing in school (if I don't try, I won't fail), which keeps me from attending college or entering a highly technical trade, which significantly alters the trajectory of my entire life. Or, if I read about virtue but do not believe that it is a worthwhile pursuit,

I simply will not stick with it. Wearing a "What Would Jesus Do" bracelet is powerless if I do not believe that what Jesus proposed is the most sublime model for the living of a human life. For most young Marines and soldiers, a more accurate bracelet might say "What Would Sergeant Major Do." We *believe* in the Sergeant Major. Beliefs strongly held, even when not intrinsically true, become self-fulfilling prophesies, in the positive or negative. I will behave as though a thing is true even when it is not and vice versa. Belief far deeper than the level of "conviction" is more powerful than the strongest willpower.

Strike the phrase "I can't" from your lexicon because you don't know if you "can't." We have no idea what we're capable of until we've applied ourselves consistently for 100 years. Often, when I say "I can't" it simply means that "I won't" because I don't believe.

Additionally, despite the subjective machinations of various strains of academic philosophy, some things are *real*, they exist regardless of what we think of them or if we think of them at all, and we have access to a body of knowledge that will attest. We must, through guided effort and relentless pursuit, come to know as much as possible about reality, including those realities that may be invisible, particularly the ones produced through virtue.

The What: *Consistency is the Prime Variable.* Consistency trumps intensity. Play the long game. The Sucker's Folly is when short-term gain obscures risk and long-term cost. An all-at-once mentality fails to achieve the proper reordering of life necessary to establish perpetual betterment. It fails at the systemic level. The deliberate life requires a daily rhythm devoted to things that matter. First, you must know what matters to you. Second, you must dedicate time to those things. You are not too busy; you waste too much time. The average American crams in like 30 hours of TV a week. Spending one hour a day on something for five years results in mastery. Making use of morning time has proven for me to be most effective. I am rarely disrupted from 4 a.m. to 8 a.m. During those quiet hours every day, I am free to learn, train, practice, and eat something healthy, if I choose.

By the time I step into the workday, where I will adjust and pivot to the demands of things outside my control, I have already girded myself with a dose of substance. The psychological edge this affords cannot be underestimated. Over time, my mornings stack up. Maybe I've read a bunch of interesting books, written a book, learned to center down, am fitter, or have learned another language. The activities and the progress are of far less importance than an ambient sense of belonging and being an active participant in life. If I'm patient and consistent, I get better.

NFL Hall of Famer Jerry Rice said, "Today I will do what others won't, so tomorrow I can do what others can't." Consistency applies also to resisting the urge to jump from one fad to another, whether diet, fitness, self-help, social, or professional. The time-tested and battle-proven fundamentals of any practice often require years to master. Immerse yourself. Often, it's user error, not flawed programming, that short-circuits success. Don't get fancy. Be patient. Be relentless. Pick a solid method and stick with it. As an old friend of mine, The Snowman, once told me, "Only boring people get bored." Water is stronger than rock.

In physical training, we reference the value of putting "miles on muscles." Young people can get strong and fast, but the man who trains over decades is a different animal. It makes you sturdy and tough to your core, mentally and physically. You develop a high pain tolerance, which makes living easier. Life is painful. Comfort with pain makes life more tolerable. You can remain functional when things get hard. You're a more useful human being.

Pavel Tsatsouline, Chairman of StrongFirst, Inc., is a Belarusian-born fitness instructor who introduced SPETSNAZ training techniques from the former Soviet Union to U.S. Special Operations forces and the American public. He is the man who brought the "kettlebell" to the U.S. Pavel uses volume and prescriptive movement as tools to forge "a hard man with hard mileage". His programs are eloquently simple and shockingly effective. There is no substitute for putting in the miles—on the road, in the gym, in the library, or at your desk.

General Eisenhower said plans are useless, but planning is indispensable. The best plans do not survive first contact with the enemy. The enemy gets a vote. If it can go wrong, it will. Do not expect your initial plan to survive. This is why New Year's Resolutions so rarely work. Gyms are full in January, but the crowd thins out by March. I resolved to get fit but didn't account for the 30-minute commute. My gym is too far away to train every day. There's not enough time. Lies. Either get up earlier, find a gym closer to your house, or buy a kettlebell and train in your yard. If you can't afford a kettlebell, use a cinder block. The ability to plan enables a leader to adjust and pivot to the conditions on the battlefield. Plan well, anticipate roadblocks, and have contingency plans to incorporate unforeseen obstacles into your training. Adapt and overcome. Keep moving.

One Stoic tenet is "the art of acquiescence", which Ryan Holiday captures well in *The Daily Stoic*. If you want a daily dose of Stoic wisdom, subscribe to his emails. The art of acquiescence is a philosophical-psychological mechanism aimed at accepting what occurs and not desiring it to be different. Past events are inaccessible. I cannot change them. What I can change is my perception of them. Such a device, when accurately wielded, prevents anything from happening that is contrary to my desire. Nietzsche's concept of Amor Fati, a love of fate, Holiday translates as, "Not merely to bear what is necessary, but to love it." There are two sides to this coin. If you don't enjoy it, you won't keep doing it.

The language of the heart has no age. You're better off playing basketball three times a week for years than pretending to "go to the gym" and doing it three times a month. Conversely, If I don't fully do it, I won't enjoy it. Wandering around a gym and monkeying randomly with the equipment is not a recipe for transformation. If you simply want to be able to say you "hit the gym", and bragging rights devoid of visible results are enough for you, then keep it up. You know better. Boredom and an ambient sense of futility are assured. Get into it. Learn the movements. Focus. Feel the resistance in your body and muscles. Feel yourself get stronger.

When you fully experience hard training, it becomes part of your truth. You begin to love it. Over time, it becomes you and you become it. The principle abides cognitively and spiritually. When you read a book (more on this later), understand what the author is saying, make connections with other sources and points of view, and consider your stance. What does it mean and what does it mean to you? Educate, collate, and formulate.

Get Comfortable with Discomfort. In a book I read years ago, "How to Become CEO", by Jeffrey J. Fox, I recall a chapter titled "Do Something Hard and Lonely." The author extolled the psychological advantages of rising before sunrise and engaging in strenuous activity.

Accomplishing something hard – some challenging physical activity – in the dark hours before sunlight hones an edge beyond the apparent physical benefits. Entering the office, the unit HQ, or the warehouse for work, I've been fully awake for hours. My mind, body, and systems operate at full capacity. I feel ready for anything. Observing counterparts slowly awakening to the reality of the day, I realize I'm way ahead of the pack. Physical exercise isn't the only method. Self-denial is inherently beneficial. Simply learning to tell myself "No" distances me from the masses.

Andrew Huberman studies and teaches practical ways to improve everyday life. He says that in the constellation of behavior, thought, feeling, and perception, behavior is the driver. If I want to be something different, I must do something different. I act differently, then I think differently, then I see the world through new eyes. There is, however, value in attending to how we habitually speak to ourselves. If a voice in our heads repeatedly condemns us, we believe it and act accordingly.

What I fill my mind with matters. The biblical concept of renewing my mind focuses efforts on perpetually meditating on edifying and deep truths throughout my day. Memorization of lengthy passages of life-giving quality is profound in this endeavor. Along with a practice of gratitude, covered in depth later, the mental churning of memorized text causes a shift in my perception of the world.

However, I cannot simply *think* my way to strength and freedom. I use my rational mind to choose small, beneficial actions that are within my power. My actions begin to build or change habits on my behalf. My rational mind can quietly yet sternly contradict the negative voice. Eventually, I can quiet that voice. It runs out of muster. First, I must act. The biblical apostle James says that "faith without works is dead." He said that if you want pure religion, don't run your mouth – visit orphans and widows in their affliction. Keep quiet and do something useful. Be quick to listen, slow to speak, and slow to anger. Be a doer whose acts are consecrated in the doing. Concurrently, I must devote my thought life to meditation on what is the purest good of which I can conceive.

The biblical Psalms offer examples. The word *integrity* is most often used in the context of honesty or moral uprightness. It is more sublime than that. Integrity is the *integration* of professed standards and commensurate behavior. My actions align with the words I speak and the thoughts I think. Integrity denotes the synthesis of intangible belief and concrete action. Intentions are not enough, as the pavement on the road to Hell suggests. A true intention, bolstered by deep belief and a clear decision, is powerful. Intentions that fall short were not true from the outset, but function most often like a magician's misdirection to distract observers from the trick playing out before them.

A well-lived life is not built on New Year's resolutions, spoken but discarded at the first sign of discomfort. Telling myself that "I want to be a good father" is meaningless until I consistently schedule intentional time with my kids and am dedicated to modeling the behavior I want them to emulate. The eventual state of the neglected soul is ruin. Thoughts matter. Action is the driver.

Self-denial has intrinsic value and is an action that I can routinely take toward transformation of any kind. Dallas Willard does a wonderful job of elucidating self-denial in the context of will, explaining the difference between *compulsive* will and *reflective* will. Simply, the compulsive will is, "I want what I want when I want it." Reflective will is a *self-limiting* will that discerns through reflection and decides based on what is good for all concerned. In that sense, through reflective will, I want what is best for everyone involved, myself included. Self-denial also guards against the insidious creep of complacency, bad habits, and declining capacities. Denial and exposure create discomfort. Examples are don't eat sugar, take cold showers, quit drinking alcohol, stop watching TV, or set your alarm to wake up 30 minutes earlier every day.

Every day means every day. Pick a challenge. Commit for seven days or thirty days. No exceptions. No excuses. Keep the promise you make to yourself. Observe the fortification of your will to choose. Accept the small rigor on your path to freedom, one step toward the captaincy of your soul. I used to refer to such structured blocks of self-denial as a "Hard Routine." They are much like a formal "fast", a classic spiritual discipline, except that you can either refrain from or engage in something.

A less demonstrative but equally effective method to cultivate self-discipline is intentionally delayed gratification. Throughout the day, be aware of moments when you want something. It may be that you want to rest during a workout or at your desk, or that you want to eat a snack. In the moment, simply tell yourself that you must wait. Give yourself conditions for which the act you desire is the consummation of a reward, e.g., after two more laps I'll take a five-minute rest or I'll keep working and get a snack at the top of the hour. Delayed gratification is a powerful tool to break addictions like smoking or sugar.

A chain smoker lights the next cigarette without thinking. If he or she becomes conscious and begins to delay the lighting of the next smoke for five minutes, that's a start. Once a five-minute delay is routine, make it ten

the fear, anxiety, uncertainty, and clutter of calamity. I use past wreckage to construct a bleak future that does not yet exist, wrecking my current state of perceived reality with phantoms of fear. I can choose to recognize each current moment as a future memory.

On the spot, I can intentionally draw the central truth, a glimpse of beauty, or a lesson from what unfolds before my eyes. I can begin to design my memories. The result is more and better memories and a richer and fuller life. Memories are the stories we write about ourselves. The more deeply I engage in the task at hand and the more of my six senses that are activated, the better the story. The better the story, the better my memories. The better my memories, the better my perceived life.

Mindset matters. My father, Big Bob, used to say that there is a difference between being "poor" and being "broke." Poverty is a mindset driven by fear that there is not enough. Such fear fuels hoarding, self-victimization, selfishness, and crushes generosity of spirit. Being broke is simply a condition – you are out of cash. You can be "broke" and still be generous with what you have. My self-worth is not predicated on my wallet. I can live without the irrational fear that today's scarcity equates to eternal scarcity. When I treat financial security as the fencer's sword – that without it I can't fight – I'm setting myself up for a rough go. The boxer's mentality is that self-worth and security reside within. Get creative, plan, chip away, change course, one step at a time.

There were some lean years during my childhood. My mother once had $10 and the challenge of figuring out how to provide school lunch for a week for my brother and me. She went to the grocery store. Walking around, looking for a creative solution, she found Twinkies on sale for $1/box. When we got home from school, there were five or six boxes of Twinkies on the kitchen counter. My brother was nine years old. I was ten. We went to a private school with a lot of wealthy kids who had punch cards to get food in the cafeteria. My mother sold her wedding ring to pay our tuition. We did not have punch cards. She sat us down and laid out the plan. Each day, she'd give us four Twinkies each. Our job was to trade three of the Twinkies for half a sandwich, a carton of milk, and a piece of fruit. The fourth Twinkie we could eat for dessert. My brother and I learned a lot that week, hustling. Mama Kay was broke, but she wasn't poor. At that moment, she was a boxer.

The Pareto Principle. Pareto's Principal (a.k.a. the 80/20 Rule), named after the Italian economist Vilfredo Pareto, asserts that 80% of outputs result from 20% of inputs. It is a guide rather than a precise ratio. Pareto's findings indicated the potential for a natural law. Mathematically, it holds across the typical distribution. It applies advantageously and adversely with equal consistency: 20% of my daily work activities yield 80% of my results and 20% of what I eat results in 80% of my weight gain; the top 20% of employees create 80% of a company's productivity and the bottom 20% of employees are responsible for 80% of a company's adverse actions, waste, malingering, and complaints. The top 20% make the company money and the bottom 20% cost the company money.

Pavel's training philosophy, like all masters of craft, runs toward simplicity. Pavel is an 80/20 Rule practitioner in the realm of fitness. Backed by decades of granular data from voluminous scientific testing, he can confidently identify the movements and their precisely directed execution that offer the best bang for the athlete's buck. The value of minimalistic training protocols for the warrior deployed to austere environments is evident. Staying fit requires less equipment, and less time, and can be done anywhere. Why does this matter to a suburban-dwelling accountant living in the U.S. with access to a globo-gym on every block? It matters because anything above what's *effective*, unless it's for pure enjoyment, is a waste of time and energy – the first an unrenewable commodity and the second a finite resource. It is the principle that is of importance.

Applied systematically to my life, I discovered that years of accrual create a life defined by excess. The 80/20 Rule abides. I eat too much. Most of my clothes never leave the closet. My off-road SUV is an over-engineered, costly vehicle that I use only to commute to work and the grocery store. Motivated to optimize my performance, year after year I add a new supplement to my regimen, but I never stop any of them, e.g., stockpiles of pills and powders.

Online, I amass scores of redundant or unnecessary subscriptions covertly billed to a credit card statement I rarely check. As a young man, I marveled at my grandmother's medicine cabinet. I had no idea why she took so many prescription pills. The truth was, she didn't know either. Our cognitive and physical landscapes are cluttered with superfluous things. They drain finite resources. We are weighed down, slowed down, and ground down. Identifying and eliminating such waste is a critical discipline toward liberation.[14]

The U.S. Marines, the smallest of the DoD components, historically receives about 10% of the DoD budget (last time I checked). The Marine culture is built on the foundation of doing more with less. It is a source of pride. A Marine toast, given in the reconnaissance community, includes the line "We have done so much, for so long, with so little, that we are now capable of doing anything with nothing." The USMC embodies the power of Pareto's Principle when applied with consistent discipline.

Greg Glassman, founder of CrossFit, described Fitness in 100 Words. "Eat meat and vegetables, nuts and seeds, some fruit, little starch, and no sugar. Keep intake to levels that will support exercise but not body fat. Practice and train major lifts: Deadlift, clean, squat, presses, C&J, and snatch. Similarly, master the basics of gymnastics: pull-ups, dips, rope climb, push-ups, sit-ups, presses to handstands, pirouettes, flips, splits, and holds. Bike, run, swim, row, etc, hard and fast. Five or six days per week mix these elements in as many combinations and patterns as creativity will allow. Routine is the enemy. Keep workouts

---

[14] R, Koch, *The 80/20 Principle: The Secret Of Achieving More With Less* (New York: Doubleday, 1998.

short and intense. Regularly learn and play new sports." Whether or not you agree with his fitness program, he distilled the cacophony of fitness and nutrition propaganda into its foundational elements. Eat naturally, mix it up, continue to learn, and have fun.

Transformation looks much like a boxer preparing for a prize fight. There is a plan and there is a goal. I want to live my life at fighting weight, hone skills, prevent injury, invest in health, and subtract that which does not add value. I want to do and possess more things that matter and fewer things that do not. Addition through subtraction. In another chapter, this path to freedom is covered in detail – *Via Negativa.*

Psychology 101 - I Can't Know Where I'm Going if I Don't Know Where I Am

> It seems to me that the basic facts of the psyche undergo a very marked alteration in the course of life, so much so that we could almost speak of a psychology of life's morning and a psychology of its afternoon. As a rule, the life of a young person is characterized by a general expansion and a striving towards concrete ends; and his neurosis seems mainly to rest on his hesitation or shrinking back from this necessity. But the life of an older person is characterized by a contraction of forces, by the affirmation of what has been achieved, and by the curtailment of further growth. His neurosis comes mainly from

his clinging to a youthful attitude which is now out of season.[15]

Psyche means *soul*. A psychologist might be a *soulologist*, were it not for the misplaced insistence that psychology governs itself by the empirical rules of science and medicine. At its roots, psychology began with a German physician named Wilhelm Wundt who predicated his nascent study of the psyche on measurable attributes, a limiting approach when observing something as complex, intangible, and invisible as the human soul. Recalling that "The soul is that dimension of the person that connects all of the other dimensions so that they form one life", as defined by Willard, our psyche necessarily includes, or binds, measurable (body, emotions, behavior) and immeasurable (spirit/heart/will) aspects of the human being. Carl Jung's psychology captured my interest because it captures and contends with the whole human being, including those elements that defy direct observation and quantification.[16]

In The Riddle of the Sphinx, Oedipus is asked, "What goes on four legs in the morning, two feet at midday, and three feet in the evening?" Oedipus answered, "Man." The narrative arc of a human life is mythologically depicted in three phases. Psychologically, the same holds. Characterizing the necessary periods and understanding the nature of the passage periods between them is the key

---

[15] Carl G. Jung, 1929.
[16] G. Moon, *Becoming Dallas Willard: The Formation of a Philosopher, Teacher, and Christ Follower* (Wheaton: IVP Books, 2018), 214-215.

to answering the basic philosophical questions of becoming a "good person" and living the "good life." Wherever I currently reside on the path between cradle and grave, the choice to be a good one is mine. Nietzsche said, in effect, that goodness and utility require *long obedience in the same direction*. At each stage of life, a man identifies those expressions of himself that are effective.

He hones them and settles into life. He locks away expressions for which he can see no utility or those too unorthodox for public consumption. Along the way, the most successful men continue to adapt. They keep their knives sharp. They collect new knives on their journey. Most men are unaware that each stage of life is one leg of the journey. It is not the entire trip. Caught unawares, a man is confused when his methods are no longer effective and when his existence begins to feel meaningless. The game is rigged. The structures are hollow, unoccupied houses on a cul-de-sac. I hold up my end of the bargain only to discover that the promises are empty. I have reached the end of a stage. Another cycle has run its course. There is no turning back.

I define the transition between stages of life as "hinge periods." Hinge periods are profound. They are the most dangerous periods in a man's life and those replete with transformative opportunities. Deliberately named, they are those periods when a man feels *unhinged*, yet they are the paradoxical link between stages. Uncanny similarities between descriptions of these phases, separated by time and space, underscore an essential human truth. Hinge periods are an invitation to integrate toward *wholeness*, a word that shares a root with *holiness*. If not understood, they can also result in functional disintegration. Once a life stage has ended, triggered by a realization that it is simply one leg of the journey and not the end, the edifice around it crumbles.

The previous phase was necessary to bring me to this place, as all roads are. The nature of a road is to fork. When I am shown again an old map, one forgotten, I find my place on it far from a final destination. Where I find I have "arrived" is no destination at all. Traveling the old road is pointless. Remaining at the juncture I will eventually die. Ahead lies a road I have never traveled. These three are my choices. I can return along the way I came, reliving a vacuous pantomime, a contrived earthly theater. Second, I can languish in purgatory, looking back, afraid to push forward into the unknown. Lastly, I can take stock of where I am, prepare for the journey to come, and step into the unknown. Kierkegaard said that life can only be understood backward, but it must be lived forward. My choices: look, languish, or live. There is no turning back.

Simple Man	Hinge Period	Complex Man	Hinge Period	Enlightened Man
2-Dimensional THE PRIMAL PHASE NEED	Point of No Return Acculturation	3-Dimensional THE COGNITIVE PHASE WANT	Point of No Return Transformation	4-Dimensional INTEGRATED/SPIRITUAL PHASE DETACH
HOME "what's for dinner?"	Triggered by awareness of existential context 3-D	WORLD "why do I exist?"	Triggered by existential dissatisfaction of 3-D	HOMECOMING "what's for dinner?"
Selfish Focus	2D is "known"; 3D is "unknown"	External Focus	3D is "known"; 4D is unknown	Internal-Upward Focus
Lizard brain drives consumption		Center of Gravity in the Ego		Center of Gravity in Higher Power
eat, sleep, crap, and copulate	self-actuation; egoic construction	explore, discover, search, slay dragons	all the dragons are dead; subordination of ego; the search for the Holy Grail	realize that the Holy Grail was "here" all along
no concept of elephants	thrust into "Adulting"	eat the elephant one bite at a time	Mid-life crisis	ride the elephant
		don't just stand there, do something		don't just do something, stand there
bias toward primal consumption		bias toward action		bias toward acceptance
Lack of awareness; immediate gratification		Self-awareness: Order, control, hustle, build, amass		Self-transcendent awareness: Accept what I cannot control, steward what I have built, give generously
A life of whatever makes me feel better		A life of MORE		A life of LESS
Express emotions with no filter		Control emotions		Observe emotions
Huh?		Absolutely.		Maybe.

I owe my journeyman's understanding of these three stages to Robert A. Johnson, author of several books (*He, She, We, Transformation, Owning Your Own Shadow, and others*), and his treatment of Carl Jung's psychology. The magic is in the application. Johnson talks of "The key to the tripod", which I understand as the insertion of a fourth dimension into three-dimensional human life, e.g., the Devil into the Holy Trinity. Johnson employs the military terminology of CoG in his treatment of psychological transformation. There are many great religions, philosophies, and programs for self-improvement. They are meaningless if you can't implement them. They are almost impossible to consistently implement when done for purely selfish reasons. Even when successfully implemented, success is devoid of meaning without a higher purpose.

"Enlightenment" requires of me a sweeping realignment of my Center of Gravity (CoG), a military term meaning that characteristic, capability, or locality from which the force derives its freedom of action, physical strength, or will to fight. Carl von Clausewitz (1780-1831), a Prussian general and author of a (arguably *the*) seminal text on warfare, defined it as "the hub of all power and movement, on which everything depends." Its attack is - or should be - the focus of all operations. Realignment of my identity within that of a Higher Power or Higher Purpose means that I derive meaning from that Source and not from myself. Another way to consider that relationship is that I derive meaning *from* it first and then existentially by inviting it to act *through* me, i.e., when its Will and my will are the same.

Paradoxically, I must take *personal* responsibility by submitting my will to a higher Will which, effectively, results in taking *relational* responsibility for myself and my life. Appropriate action, what matters and what doesn't, is understood contextually. What my responsibilities are is understood through that which I serve. To understand "death to self", I rely on Willard's definition of *life* as "self-initiating, self-sustaining, and self-directing power." To lose my life is to willingly and utterly depend on the Source instead of myself to initiate, sustain, and direct my actions. When I do, I find and begin to live a new reality, a *new life*.

Personal responsibility is effective and meaningful only within the context of a set of moral absolutes. Relativism is of no value in this endeavor. A crude example of personal responsibility and discipline run amok might be a serial killer devoted to improving his craft. Behavior alteration programs, while effective in breaking bad habits and addictions, or in creating positive habits, are insufficient to produce existential freedom and bounty, the kind described in scripture as "abundant life." I can optimize my behavior to become more effective within the confines of my social and cultural domains and never derive meaning from any of it. In short, I must "get religion" lest my interminable efforts amount to little more than selecting between treadmills or, as I've heard, switching seats on the Titanic.

On Fear. When you ask people what they're afraid of, they say things like "public speaking." That's not what they're afraid of; that's the situation where the fear is triggered. I could probably boil all my fears down to a core fear: that there is no discoverable purpose in this life according to which a man must live to be deemed worthwhile, equating to a wasted life. I don't want to have lived a wasted life. That is my core fear. I'm afraid that I'll break my back working for something meaningful until I die but that it won't matter anyway. My core fear, that there is no discoverable purpose in life, is the punchline to the Cosmic Joke - the most monumental of strategic blunders.

It may seem odd to include my fear that nothing may matter in the long run. I include it because it was my fear. This book is not a direct antidote to that fear but models how I have been relieved of it through the experiential process. My practice of principles teaches me that devotion to a well-lived life is what creates a well-lived life. It is not about outcomes, and it is certainly not about perfection. *The effort itself is worthwhile.* It is the most worthwhile endeavor of which I can conceive. It has a depth and purpose to it that nothing else does. It feels as though I was created to *become* in this way. There is a spiritual quality to it.

The mindset and the actions create a well-lived life, which is its own reward. My mind questions it, but my body and my soul endorse it. To search for and to traffic with truth, to experiment and to analyze, and to put my back into the practices reveal experiential maxims. I know it is worth it because I can feel it. As such, with the faith of the acquitted, I humbly offer what follows to be used as you will.

2

Willingness to Change

"Nature of any kind thrives on forward progress. And progress for a rational mind means not accepting falsehood or uncertainty in its perceptions, making unselfish action its only aim, seeking and shunning only the things it has control over, and embracing what nature demands of it – the nature in which it participates as the leaf's nature does in the tree. Except that the nature shared by the leaf is without consciousness or reason, and subject to impediments. Whereas that shared by human beings is without impediments, rational, and just, since it allots to each an equal and proportionate share of time, being, purpose, action, and chance. Examine it closely. Not whether they're identical point by point, but in the aggregate: this weighed against that."

– Marcus Aurelius

It is not enough to make one Big Decision to rechart my course. I must be willing to make a million small decisions, moment by moment, to stay on course.

Get Your Act Together. If I learn a lot, know a lot, and do a lot, I change a lot.

On Agency and Change Agency. As toddlers, we become conscious of ourselves as sovereign entities. A toddler expresses the recognition of its agency with an exerted individual will, most often by using the word "no." When a

62

toddler says "no", they aren't being disagreeable, they are saying, "I am me. I am not you. Recognize me." Toddlers also like to say, "Mine." They are saying that they are a person and have things. Specific things belong to them, not to other people. The things are extensions of themselves. They are sifting and categorizing the world based on their discovery that they are autonomous. Once a human has recognized its unique agency, its self-consciousness becomes the center of its world. It is the first step toward ego development. Self-consciousness endures the remainder of our lives.

In immaturity, we do not rationally filter our wants and needs, nor do we consider subjecting them to the greater good. Also, as children, we have not yet learned to manage our faces. We cannot "hide" behind controlled expressions or within our bodies. We lack the tools to accomplish this. Untempered feelings and desires are on display. As we mature, we learn to hide, but our feelings remain the same unless we choose to do something about them. Self-will and self-obsession are at the heart of dysfunction.

When emotional maturity does not temper our "selfness", the result is calamitous. I am my worst problem. Most of my problems stem from selfishness. Paradoxically, I am also the solution to my problems. I am the problem, and I am the solution. I must get over myself. I cannot get over myself by myself. The antidote to self-obsession is self-awareness followed by self-denial. I must become willing to honestly inventory and address patterns of thought and behavior that are not functional, healthy, or in my best interest as a worthwhile human being. I must be willing to accept full blame for my current condition and the tone of my life. The limits of what I can control I embody. I cannot control what happens, but I can control how I respond to it (though not how I *react*; reactions occur without thought and are only changed through conditioning). I cannot control how you speak to me, but I can control how I speak to you and how I respond or don't respond to your words. I cannot control other people's behavior, but I can set clear boundaries around what I will and will not accept. I teach others how to treat me. I attract what I most am. Dysfunction attracts dysfunction. Addiction attracts addiction. Chaos attracts chaos.

Willingness to change starts with accepting that you are 100% responsible for yourself and for your life: past, present, and future. If there is anyone to blame, blame yourself or don't blame at all. Things are the way they are. See reality clearly. See yourself clearly. What do you want to change? Are you willing to do hard things to make that change? If you are satisfied with how things are, look no further. Congratulate yourself and keep on trucking. Be cool and hang out. If you're not satisfied, you must determine the part you play in the creation of that condition. You must focus only on your part and decide whether you will do something about it. Are you willing to pay a price to be free of unconscious forces in your life?

The willingness to change does not require a willingness to overturn your entire life. That comes later. There are significant improvements to be made by homing in on a single limiting factor or inferior function and devoting energy toward its improvement. A simple framework for reducing complexity is to focus on two things: start one thing and stop one thing. Building one new healthy habit and stopping one unhealthy habit gives you plenty to do, it narrows your focus, and it helps you resist the urge to be impatient. Many of us, once we realize that we want to make changes, are swept up in the energy and excitement. We want to fix everything at once. We want to make up for lost time. The beginning of wisdom is a firm grasp of the obvious. Change can be painful, and it can take time. Relax. Make a start. Do one thing at a time.

Change starts with you. You cannot fix what you refuse to face. It starts in your mind, with your body, and in your home. Jordan Peterson offers practical advice along these lines. Changing the world begins with cleaning your room. If I cannot run an orderly household, why do I consider myself qualified to weigh in on world events? In short, if I can't manage myself, I am unqualified to manage anyone else. I am the problem. You are the problem. Focus on the problem. Anything else is justification, projection, excuses, manipulation, or misdirection. Knock it off and own your shit.

"There is a principle which is a bar against all information, which is proof against all argument, and which cannot fail to keep a man in everlasting ignorance. This principle is contempt prior to examination."

– Rev. William Poole, 1879.

How Our Brains Work. All human communication is interpretation and translation. My interpretation of the world ignites my feelings. My feelings drive my thoughts and behavior. When I write, I don't necessarily write what's true or real. I translate what I observe. I interpret it. I listen to the world around me and I write what I hear. I observe and describe what I see, inherently limited by my observational and interpretive abilities, and filtered through personal experiential bias. That translation is my voice.

This phenomenon engenders ideas like "relative truth", "emotional truth", or "my truth." The danger of individualized truth is that it is inherently unreliable. My interpretation of my life now and the realities of historical human experience are not necessarily the same thing. I must have principles against which to qualify my interpretations. Enduring stories, religion, philosophy, human testimony, and psychology provide persistent and *overlapping* themes crucial to evaluating my interpretations.

If I am to discover truth or reality through observation, I am only able through appropriate context, i.e., *knowledge*. Historical wisdom around fundamental themes of humanity provides a rubric. Thoughtful examination requires testing my "truths" to determine if they conform to nature, as the Stoics would say. Do my "truths" stand to reason, are my interpretations filtered through the wisdom of collective human experience, and do they remain "true" if stripped of emotions? Husserl's phenomenology asserts that there are "things" that exist and are *real*, which are independent of human thought or observation, and this body of "things" includes the invisible and intangible, such as virtue, moral knowledge, and, yes, even the kingdom of the heavens. It is realism that interacts most directly with our common notions of the mystical.

Willard was a Husserlian philosopher and spent a lifetime working this out. I am not a formally trained philosopher, so don't take my word for it, but the meaning I extricate is that there exists a reality beyond that which I can see, and that self-denial is the path to experience such a life, that is inaccessible through direct effort (hence the need for disciplined practice), and to access a power that transcends direct human willpower alone. The power to forgive someone who has severely harmed me is one such example. Another is the power to accurately predict a future event or to receive a warning in a dream. Acceptance that there exist *real things* that I can observe and experience, that are beyond my power, and that there are non-subjective (objective) absolutes, inspires me to gain knowledge from which to base action.

Our brains are wired so that we can only concentrate on one thing (maybe two = genius!) at a time. The rest runs on programmed neurological constellations, chunked patterns that create an automated habit (Duhigg) for almost everything we repeatedly do. Like psychological *schema*, the experience-based preconceptions our brains use subconsciously to organize and interpret new information, both run on autopilot and govern the bulk of what we do and think. *The secret to discipline without discipline is the rewriting of habit patterns* (Kahneman). *The secret to seeing the world through new eyes is to rewrite schema.* The one thing on which we focus, and to which we put our hands, is the One Thing. The One Thing is also the narrow gate to heaven. In physical fitness training, my rule is that there is "only ever one rep." The only repetition that exists is the one I'm doing. It's the only rep that ever matters. A rep resides within a set, a set within a series, a series within a daily session, a day within an intentional program, and the program is derived from principles collated to achieve specific outcomes. The curation of training principles is strategy; the program is operations; and the reps are the physical tactical expression of strategic imperatives. Mastering the art of full concentration on a single rep is the Rosetta Stone of simplifying change and the portal to the richest version of my life. I refer to this as the One Rep Method (ORM).

In *Thinking, Fast and Slow*, Daniel Kahneman, winner of the Nobel Prize in Economics, illustrates in depth the functions of the two human mental systems, 1) involuntary (fast), and 2) voluntary (slow). Automated habit is a function of System 1, along with a host of mental functions we rarely consider, like depth perception, facial expressions, detection of a person's vibes, sensing danger, and sixth sense moments. System 2 acts as a conscious governor over the impulsive System 1, analyzes complexity and operates on a budget. We have a finite amount of energy and space from which to muster targeted mental activity. Working in concert, these two systems can make it feel like I'm consciously doing multiple things at once – ref. the overused and misunderstood idea of "multitasking" – like driving, navigating with the on-screen map, talking on the phone, and finishing my coffee. The reality is that the bulk of activity in that scenario runs on automatic, driven by neurological programs that govern repeated activities (operating the vehicle, drinking coffee). I do those things without thinking about them, so I'm not multitasking at all. Computers multitask, humans do not.

When I hear someone say that they're "multitasking", what I hear is "I look busy but I'm not getting anything accomplished." Back to the driving scenario, System 2 skips from my phone conversation to the map and back again but is continually diverted to process and interpret fresh inputs as I drive through a new part of town or encounter traffic. The result is that I am certain to miss parts of the phone conversation and I may miss the next exit if I don't allocate my limited mental resources appropriately.

The One Rep method is to prioritize the focus of System 2 and do one thing. Akin to overeating during the holidays, I tend to tax System 2 to the limits of its capacity, fragmenting the power of my full attention. Under the misconception that activity and productivity are directly proportional, and the deeper delusion that productivity is the point, I unwittingly short-circuit my cognitive powers. In attempting to do everything, I find that little gets done. Or, very little ever has my full attention, leading to many things partially or poorly done.

Parkinson's Law states that untended demand will increase to meet available supply. I don't eat until I'm satisfied, I eat until my plate is clean. Central governments perpetually increase in size, programs endure past their usefulness, and budgets are rewarded when spent but penalized when saved. *Viola*, the proverbial "self-licking ice cream cone." Doing One Thing is as simple as eliminating competing activities from the focus of System 2, paying more attention to the primary activity I'm doing, and leaving mental resources available for recruitment, rest, or creative epiphanies. It's a kind of intentional mental resource budgeting, spending cognitive shekels on necessary and important things, but keeping some in savings. When I choose to do one thing – navigate to a new part of town, without distraction – I am amazed by what I experience.

The navigation itself goes much more smoothly and I also have the mental space to notice things around me. Assuming I don't squander available mental horsepower masticating my to-do list or inventorying the perceived tragedies and injustices of my life, I am free to take it all in. I notice interesting buildings, read the names of streets, notice a man in a fedora smoking a cigar, and feel the energy of the area. I experience the environment as I move through it in a way that feels like discovery. My curiosity quickens. I am likely to remember much of it. As a bonus, I don't lose my way. The point is not to increase the effectiveness or the quality of my work, though those are collateral benefits. Instead, the aim is to invest more deeply into the task at hand to unlock the beauty, complexity, and mystical qualities inherent in the mundane.

Kahneman explains that when System 2 "endorses" a suggestion, those become beliefs and spurn voluntary action. Most of what we "think and do originates in ... System 1, but System 2 takes over when things get difficult, and it normally has the last word" (25). It's an efficient and (typically) effective relationship. However, System 1 creates situational models based on experience, which include intrinsic biases that lead to errors. Moreover, System 2 is hard-wired to economize effort. If left untended, it defaults to laziness. These manifest in unfettered opinionating as biased babble delivered as fact. I hear something that is automatically filtered through System 1 and, if System 2 doesn't take the time (expend the energy) to evaluate it, it becomes a belief (fact) based on the knowledge and experience of a sample size of one. If I care about a topic, especially a complex one, I have a duty to understand it lest I formulate a reckless opinion. I must recognize how my brain works. I bring a healthy dose of skepticism to my impressions.

This requires effort. Understanding includes collecting information from the opposing sides of the debate. It also includes considering a topic within a historical context. Finally, taking a stance remains inherently biased. As I "objectively" collect data and process information, I interpret it by running it through the filter of my own experience. Subconsciously, my belief system renders value judgments. Even my most intentionally considered opinions remain suspect. Being thoughtfully biased is preferable to being unconsciously biased.

STFU. You have the right to hold an opinion. Do not confuse this with the right to share your opinion. Zach Bryan sang in "Burn, Burn, Burn" that "everyone seems a damn genius lately, Tik-Tok talking..." People talk too much. More precisely, in day-to-day life, people talk too much about things they do not understand or lazily parrot what they have heard others say without examination. I'm guilty of it. This is our current one-dimensional, byte-sized version of civilized conversation.

As such, it amounts to recycled, insubstantial trivia. In post-post-post-modern Western culture, or whatever era we find ourselves currently enduring, we might call the Information Age the "Data Inundation Age." Data becomes information when it's interpreted. The ubiquitous tide of news, ideas, arguments, politics, and the banal trivia of people's lives posted on social media is more often data than information. My friend in Kentucky posts a picture of herself in a diner eating a Philly Cheesesteak. Is it data or information? It's factual because the picture offers proof that she was served a sandwich and that she was physically present in the diner. Absent context, I cannot derive meaning from the picture, though it might make me hungry.

Relevance and value require interpretation. The typical Western life is a non-stop flow of low-density trifles. Absent scrutiny, trifles don't qualify as information. Subjected to scrutiny, they evaporate. There's too much of it to contend with intellectually and most of it is unworthy of consideration. This does not hamper the sharing of unqualified opinions. The right to hold an opinion does not inherently qualify the opinion. Some opinions are worth more than others e.g., the "expert" opinion or the findings of multiple peer-reviewed blind studies. I know and care little about most things. I speak significantly less when I limit myself to sharing only those opinions on matters that I have thoroughly considered and taken an informed stance. Habitually sharing unqualified opinions is intellectually lazy.

I read somewhere that, "Great minds discuss ideas, average minds discuss current events, and small minds gossip about people." A tenured philosophy professor, a clinical psychologist, or an Ivy League theologian might read this book and disagree or epistemologically eviscerate my assertions on a given topic with a hurricane of knowledge and experience that I do not possess. The point I intend to make is that to "qualify" an opinion, and more so to justify a belief, I do not have to know *everything*, and I must remain receptive to correction, but I must do my best to consciously consider, to think through, and to bounce against a trusted body of knowledge any matter of importance. Moreover, I must put a thing to the test in my life to determine if it stands up to experience. I'm not concerned about knowing the "right" answer on a test but about a principle's effectiveness. *Does it work in real life?*

In the military, staff officers and non-commissioned officers conduct what is known as a Commander's Update Brief, "the CUB." CUBs take many forms, from informal stand-ups to drawn-out, formal PowerPoint briefs from each staff section while seated around a horseshoe-shaped conference table in a stuffy, overcrowded room. They can be painful. Among staff officers, one rule abides: "Push to talk, not to think."

When it's your turn to deliver your brief, know what you're going to say *before* you start talking. Don't think out loud. A formal CUB is already too long. When a staff officer isn't prepared and stumbles through a brief, it raises questions. The Commander probes. Probing takes time. Don't be the jackass who shows up unprepared and exacerbates what is already an endurance exercise. Do your job and don't screw everybody else over. Keep things moving. Be brief, be brilliant, and be gone. The principle holds in life. Unless you have thoroughly thought through a topic, and understand it from multiple objective angles, keep your opinion to yourself unless it is directly solicited. Consuming another person's time with trifling nonsense, often against their will, is disrespectful. My arrogance or ignorance is directly proportional to my willingness to waste your time with my drivel.

Wendler said that being fat, lazy, and ignorant isn't a good role model. I do not respect myself when I am those things. Like the ocean erodes the shoreline, my propensity to be fat, lazy, and ignorant laps ceaselessly at the shore of my subconscious. I earn self-respect when I take action to resist my tendencies toward erosion. In combat triage, the first order of business is often to stop the bleeding. Only after a medic stops the bleeding can he or she render follow-on aid. Once stabilized, a medical team can begin to infuse healing and strengthening protocols to fortify the patient's lifeblood. If I analyze my current condition, I may find hemorrhaging. I start by identifying habits or behaviors that are sucking the lifeblood out of me. I stop those first. Once I create stability in my life by eliminating my worst dysfunctions, I can begin to add healthy habits.

I am free to visualize the person I want to be. I require unobstructed vision to identify the gap between where I am and where I want to be. However, the vision will not sustain the required effort over time. Reference the New Year's Resolution. Big Bob used to tell me to wish in one hand and spit in the other to see which hand would fill up first. The essential question is not whether I want to be virtuous, fit, or educated. Once I have specifically defined what my goal is, the pivotal question is, "Am I willing to pay the price?" If I'm not willing to trade comfort for improvement, my dreams remain dreams.

Regardless, I will pay some price. The cost of discipline is negligible compared to the cost of untended entropy. If I ignore my health, I will pay a larger sum in pain and misery than the small discomforts of discipline. Likewise, ignorance is costly, both in mistakes and lost opportunity. Jocko Willink sums up the "Striving to be an eminently qualified human" with this maxim, "Unmitigated daily discipline in all things. It is the only way." He outlines "The Code", "The Evaluation", and "The Protocols." It is a simple and effective framework for envisioning my ideal, evaluating myself across functional areas, and implementing protocols to address gaps in health and to handle real-life scenarios. In general terms, I decide that I want to be "better at life." Great! What does that look like? Envision your ideal self who is speaking, acting, and being in each functional area, e.g., at work, with your spouse, with your kids, with your family and friends, around your home, as a strong, healthy man or woman living their most effective life. Break it down into parts. What actions benefit me toward becoming that man or woman? What actions hinder me?

Changing behaviors requires discipline. Discipline is what enables me to achieve through indirect effort what I cannot achieve through direct effort (Willard). Discipline is the consistent accomplishment of small actions, the sum of which produces demonstrable change. That is the price. The price is 1,000s of moments of self-denial, 1,000s of small wins instead of one big win, and 1,000s of moments of doing what others won't so that you can do what others can't.

Most people aren't willing to pay the price. Everybody seems to want "better", "more", or "less", but they'll sacrifice very little to make it happen. Average people don't commit. Mediocre people eat life's leftovers and call it Fate or bad luck. To be clear, mediocrity is not a determination based on comparing myself to others. I am mediocre when I fail to optimize *my* potential and when I settle for a half-baked version of *myself*. We can all do better and be better. If I refuse to work toward improvement, I accept a lesser self and the disappointment of letting myself down. If this attitude persists long enough, I consider myself to be inadequate because I am. The recognition of my inadequacies is not self-flagellation. I'm not "shaming" myself. Self-shaming is conflating an inadequacy in one area with total inadequacy as a human being. It is also used to create a label I can use to skirt the truth. Labeling the calling out of inadequacy as "bad," I justify lowering my standards to meet my behavior, instead of improving my behavior to meet my standards. I need the truth.

Untended, I will devolve mentally, physically, emotionally, and spiritually until I no longer recognize myself. No decision is a decision. Stockdale said, "I must never confuse the faith that I will prevail in the end, which I cannot afford to lose, with the courage to face the brutal facts of my current reality."

Discipline is a Muscle. The more you use it, the stronger it becomes. Discipline is transferable. When I learn discipline in one area of my life, I can apply that strength to other areas. The "start one-stop one" technique enables me to reduce all the possible things to "this" and "that" specifically. If I can discipline myself to start one thing and to stop one thing, I've made a beginning. Flexing that muscle feels good. The more I do it the more I want to do it. Kahneman identifies a phenomenon called "ego depletion." "Activities that impose high demands on System 2 require self-control, and the exertion of self-control is depleting and unpleasant."[18] It presents as a loss of motivation (reference every failed New Year's Resolution!).

---

[18] D, Kahneman, *Thinking, Fast and Slow* (New York: Farrar, Straus, and Giroux, 2011), 42.

He goes on to describe how the nervous system consumes massive amounts of glucose when taxed, equivalent to running sprints. To be able to recover quickly from sprints, I must run sprints. Continual practice in self-control, i.e., self-discipline, improves my capacity to exert self-control and speeds my recovery from the effort. When done repeatedly and consistently, it deepens neurological grooving and becomes automatic.

This is "discipline without discipline." I set out on a new path. In the beginning, it requires a great deal of effort to stay on the path. It gets easier. One day, I walk that path automatically. I no longer must think about it or force myself to do it. I do it because it's *what I do*. At this phase of development, I free cognitive resources to spend on other things.

In the addiction recovery world, they say that pain is the price of admission into a new life. Procrastination is sloth in five syllables. I must stop merely wanting things and start doing things. If it was easy, everyone would do it. *Trying* is not enough. Choose between character and comfort. Epictetus asked, "How long are you going to wait before you demand the best for yourself?" An outside force must disrupt inertia.

You are unique, but you are not special. My personality, my preferences, and my worldview do not exclude me from the laws of nature. I will get out what I put in. I will reap what I sow. All structures are unstable over time. I cannot pretend for long. I must become or be found out.

Suffer in silence. Doing hard things and boring everyone in your life with a play-by-play of your self-sacrificial journey short-circuits one of the primary benefits. Often, this ploy is a cover-up story veiled as justification to make it seem like you're putting in the effort when there's nothing to show for it. Doing uncomfortable things and not talking about them is sometimes tough. When I dedicate myself to a path and muster the discipline to stay on it, I feel proud of myself. Sometimes I want to share that. Sharing it does not always inspire others.

People close to me may not want to feel "inferior" when I become willing to change but they are not, as though my desire to improve is a reflection of their shortcomings. Or maybe they simply don't care, which is understandable. Get over it. Observable positive change in another is often inspiring. Insubstantial monologuing is boring. Bragging is rarely well-received, and it devalues my efforts by treating them as if they need external affirmation. Legitimate effort does not require affirmation. It stands on its own. Its value is intrinsic. Respect others enough to let the results tell the story. It's a mind game. Do the work, let it speak for itself, and harden up.

Two effective models for curbing your tongue are: 1) Ask yourself three questions in the following order: a) Does it need to be said, b) Does it need to be said now, and c) Does it need to be said by me (J.D. Crow), and 2) Is what I'm about to say more beautiful than silence? Things said cannot be unsaid. Be ruthlessly editorial with the 1,000s of thoughts that run through your mind every day. Save the energy of System 2 for the things that matter. Consider those things thoroughly, focusing on one idea at a time. Do not allocate mental resources to trivial things.

Let trivia come and go, observed but not captured. Save your brain power for what counts. In the meantime, recognize that half of what you think you know is biased, and the other half is noise. Aurelius describes the citadel of one's soul, our inner getaway. He suggests brief moments of retreat within to renew yourself. He asks, what exactly is there to complain about? People? He suggests we consider that most people don't make mistakes intentionally, to remember the vast numbers who have fought with each other and are now gone, that we ultimately exist for each other, and "keep your mouth shut."

Do I complain about my fate, my situation, my body, my reputation? Remember how quickly we all are forgotten. Take the "back roads of yourself. Above all, no strain, and no stress. Be straightforward. Look at things like a man, a human being, a citizen, a mortal" (Aurelius, 31-32). Be hard on yourself but go easy on others. Be a lady; be a gentleman; keep quiet about it.

If You Work Hard You can be an Astronaut (and other lies our mothers tell us). In her book <u>Radical Candor</u>, Kim Scott unpacks a concept she calls "ruinous empathy." Ruinous empathy is the well-intentioned avoidance of honest feedback to protect feelings. In the long run, it does more harm than good. If my boss doesn't tell me what I need to improve, and I'm blind to it, I don't find out until the day I get fired. "Why didn't you tell me?" *Deliberately avoiding necessary unpleasantness or skirmishes to keep* *the peace ensures eventual war or collapse.* I was a reasonably smart kid. My mother told me that I could do anything. I believed her.

At forty, a therapist asked me what my "superpower" was. I answered, "I can do anything I set my mind to." He laughed. He asked if I could jump from the top of the key and dunk a basketball. I thought about it. "No, I couldn't do that right now." "Right now?", he asked. "What if I gave you a year to train for it?" I thought more. "I'm not sure. I honestly don't know if I could ever do that. I doubt it. No, there's no way." My therapist smiled. He said, "Your superpower is that you *think* you can do anything. That's a source of power. It's also your greatest weakness because you can't." Our greatest strengths and weaknesses are often two sides of one coin.

Dishonesty is a form of disrespect. I don't tell you the truth because I don't give you enough credit. I don't think you can handle it. I *protect* you from the truth. In the long run, I'm of no use to you as a catalyst for growth. My standard is not what I expect from you, it's what I tolerate from you. In professional settings, the quality of work and a person's work ethic can often be quantified, or at least qualified, in concrete ways. It's potentially easier to offer direct and clear feedback in those scenarios. But bosses rarely do. In personal relationships, it is muddier. In both cases, pulling punches and avoiding negative feedback results in a dishonest dynamic.

The most significant relationship that suffers from ruinous empathy is the relationship we have with ourselves. I'm simultaneously too hard on myself and too easy. I beat myself up on repeat with self-doubt and disparagement, but I let myself off the hook for failing to simply do my best. The pendulum swings from self-flagellation to "I can do anything!" I need to have a sit down with myself, pour myself a cup of coffee, and get real. I'm not a saint and I'm not a Hell's Angel.

I'm not a worthless human being nor am I a demi-god. I'm capable of doing good work, but if I want to keep my job I need to start showing up on time. I can't blame my weight gain on "bad genetics" when I eat dessert five nights per week. My inability to control my temper is not because my parents spanked me when I was a kid. My behavior now is my fault. I get the credit and I get the blame. When I am calm, rational, and honest with myself, I can begin to take responsibility for my actions, regardless of where I came from and where I am. Once I learn to do it with myself, I can learn to do it with you. Only then can I become a true friend.

My reality is that I cannot do *anything*. Recognizing this is liberating when it leads to the question, "What *can* I do?" I soon learn that there are many things I can do to improve my station. When I boil my areas of dysfunction and undeveloped areas of inferior function into elements, I realize that I can do "this" and I can do "that" to make improvements. Enough "this" and "that" add up to a lot over time. In Transformation, "We are so materialistic and so enamored of the power of human will that we refuse to relinquish what is irretrievably out of our reach." In context, Johnson is discussing the American ideal of perpetual youth and the problems associated with our ideas of the "unlived life."[19] Johnson's solution to this conundrum is not a *literal* one.

Beyond considerations of perpetual youth, I have harnessed the willpower to accomplish many things. For decades, I relied on it. Centered in my ego, my willpower was the engine that could. Encountering periods of life devoid of purpose and bereft of motivation, willpower is not enough to sustain me. Purpose fuels will. Without purpose, the fumes are not enough to sustain sheer willpower. The appropriate use of willpower requires alignment with a higher purpose. Otherwise, it runs riot or runs out of fuel, experienced as flameouts or fiery crashes.

I cannot rely on willpower alone to make sweeping or long-lasting changes. It is a finite resource. I must reduce "changes" to the next action, one action at a time, and employ willpower toward focused effort. Revisiting the stages of human life, Johnson would argue that willpower is essential to a successful 3-dimensional life but is inadequate for evolution to a 4-dimensional life. A strong will is a useful tool when applied appropriately. It is not a solution to many of the most important things in life, nor is it a substitute for purpose.

Big Bob once muttered, "I'd like to buy her for what she's worth and sell her for what she thinks she's worth." My self-delusion is theatrical. If I want to get clean, I must come clean. A close friend of mine reduced the entire

---

[19] Johnson, 68.

program of Alcoholics Anonymous to "Take Stock, Clean House, and Help Others." The dilemma of my self-delusion is that I think I need things that I don't, and I don't think I need things that I do. It's like throwing darts from a merry-go-round.

I continually miss the dartboard and complicate my dysfunction or shallow capacity by thinking that I need to learn more about the aerodynamics of darts, Kentucky windage, environmentally-driven launch-trajectory offsets, and barometric compensations so that I can hit the board. What I need to do is get off the merry-go-round, but I don't realize that I'm on it. I'm bewildered by perpetual dizziness. I continue to miss the board and lose darts, but I don't stop throwing them. I won't give up! I won't give in! Where there's a will there's a way! Bono sang it, "How long? How long will we sing this song?"

In *Stop Walking on Eggshells*, authors Paul Mason and Randi Kreger recount a story. Paraphrased, a Zen disciple sits down to tea with his Master. The Zen Master holds a stick and says, "If you drink your tea, I will hit you with this stick. If you do not drink your tea, I will hit you with this stick. What will you do?" When I'm too close to a situation, my own especially, dilemmas present options where there are seemingly no good choices. If I step back, there is what C.S. Lewis referred to as the "third option", that which is not immediately evident when stifled in a dilemma between two options. In this case, the third option is to take away the Master's stick.

Cultivating a willingness to change requires courage and patience to take stock honestly and thoroughly. It is not an overnight matter. It is rarely the result of a life-changing epiphany. Rather, it is a lifelong endeavor, what mystical traditions and religions across the ages refer to as a chosen path or *way*. I must know what I want and why I want it. Both digging to the roots of authentic human expression and understanding that which conforms to natural laws is akin to a massive archaeological dig.

It is to be done with order, progression, and care. What we unearth are clues, not necessarily answers. From the clues we conduct forensics, identify trends, and compare those with a body of knowledge bolstered intentionally to provide a backdrop of context and understanding. Without relational context, what we discover about ourselves may answer the "what" but will rarely answer the "why."

Nobody Likes a Quitter. When two drinking buddies are relaxing with some cold pops, and one of them gets real by confessing to the other that he's considering cutting back on drinking or stopping altogether, the other one says, "Nobody likes a quitter." It's humorous. They both chuckle. The first one has a decision to make. He was not joking when he confessed. There is a chance he hoped his buddy might agree or might volunteer to join him. They could quit together. Let's team up and get healthy! Neither wants to lose the other's friendship. They won't admit that their relationship is built around drinking together. They may not realize it. But there is a gnawing sense – *a knowing* – that the dynamic will not survive intact if one of them quits. When a person gets serious about getting healthy, he or she will be faced with hard decisions. Relationships are one example. What happens when my spouse has a sweet tooth and I decide to quit eating sugar? Or I decide that I watch too much TV, but my spouse considers TV watching to be "quality time" together.

Or I become intentional with time management at work and resist disruptions by co-workers. I begin to block out focused time during my day for things that matter, so I don't respond quickly to messages or social media. People think there is something wrong with me or that I'm mad at them when I don't respond quickly enough. The ability to draw new boundaries around your commitments is vital. Old boundaries don't serve new commitments. Plan for sacrifice. Understand the price you are willing to pay. Be prepared with firm but kind answers for people who will not understand and will (un)intentionally test you.

Many won't notice, some will challenge you, some may lash out, and some will be genuinely interested and supportive. You will be confronted with choices. You must know where you stand and you must assign a clear value to your efforts. When I know what a thing is worth, it is easier to place value on other things in comparison.

Such conscious comparison enables prioritization and filtering. Watching an extra episode of my favorite series is not as valuable to me as taking an after-dinner walk with my wife. Staying up late for no reason is not as valuable to me as doing my early morning workout. _____ is not as valuable to me as _____ [fill in the blanks]. I must not allow potential external conflict with others to serve as an excuse to give up or to cheat myself. I may tell myself that I ate the donut to avoid hurting someone else's feelings, but, come on. The more I trim away the overgrowth of competing interests and conflicting habits, the easier it becomes to walk my chosen path freely.

Thoreau said, "All good things are wild and free." Willard asked the fundamental questions on life: What is reality? What is a good life? Who is a good human? What keeps me from being and living the good versions? What stands in my way? To be a good man I must be a free one. *I imprison myself.* I must learn to do fewer unimportant things and invest more in things that matter. When I intentionally do less, I do more. I must *become* fewer things to more people and deeper, more meaningful things to fewer people. When I am intentionally less, I am wonderfully more.

By continuing to read, you are signing a "cost-plus" contract. In construction, a cost-plus contract captures known costs and allows for ambiguous flexibility. You enter it having an idea of the costs, but there will be surprises and, ultimately, it will cost more, or you will spend more in unexpected areas than predicted. The target moves. You can't have everything. There will be trade-offs.

If you can accept this level of ambiguity and have decided that enough is enough, it's time to arm you with baseline knowledge. You must focus and learn by using the primers in this book to expand your research into needed areas. You will decide what you need more of and what you need less of for your own best interest. Focused effort will result in a personalized plan. Once you have a plan, you must decide if you will commit to it. Knowledge first, then a plan, then commitment.

3

Intense Focus – Learn and Plan

Don't Mind the Mule, Load the Wagon. Stop wasting energy caring about what other people think or do. Focus on what you think and do – that's what matters.

Aristotle said, "Education is an ornament in prosperity and a refuge in adversity." Remember my comments on autodidacticism from earlier. Self-educate. I'll cover topics vital to me but pay special attention to your ideas while reading. The purpose of this book is to introduce ideas that have mattered to me, but I am not equipped to do justice to the scope and depth of them.

The books or thinkers that I reference are experts or specialists of some kind. I am neither an expert nor a specialist. I have been able to mine from the wisdom of others valuable knowledge that has served me in real ways, at the level of living. In any case, go to the source. Cultivate curiosity. If you have a question, look it up. Don't believe what I tell you. Discover for yourself. Go down rabbit holes. See what other people have written on topics that interest you. Be aware of the things that touch you most, especially those that elicit a strong emotional response. You are getting to know yourself. You will not always like what you learn. Keep at it. Take notes. Begin a journal to capture ideas, questions, and lists for further exploration. Put ideas in your own words so that you can understand and remember them. Look for how you relate to a topic, in either healthy or unhealthy ways. Feel it. Start learning and never stop.

Of particular importance, being a boxer is not a "results-oriented" mindset. Sheer willpower is sufficient to produce certain results, at certain times, but the systemic cost makes them unsustainable and, at times, unrepeatable. How long can you *force* yourself to do something? Instead of thinking in terms of results, e.g., a quantified one-time outcome, think in terms of growth as it relates to conditioning or capacity, e.g., "I can do this all day" when it comes to disciplined execution of next steps or selected modes of self-denial. The envelope is meant to be pushed. A new normal is simply a baseline for further growth.

Self-discipline is categorically transferrable. For example, when I become accustomed to routine fasting from food, it becomes much easier for me to endure the discomfort of a daily cold shower. I get used to not getting what I want, so not getting one thing is like not getting another thing. *It is the* conditioning *that is of primary importance, not the outcome of any single effort. From it comes the power to grow along any chosen path more effortlessly.*

I suggest to anyone embarking on a growth path to assume a long view of the effort. I think of character formation as *forging*, the intentional application of pressure, heat, or tempering over time to produce consistent incremental change. The road to character is mapped more as a trajectory than a clearly defined jaunt from point A to point B. Despite what marketing infomercials suggest, I cannot create six-pack abs in six minutes any more than I can learn neurosurgery in six weeks through online certifications. I have not found a quick fix that sticks. Forging requires patience. Character formation is not a pop culture "phenom", it does not go viral.

There are no microwaveable solutions or magic pills. Single-serving flash programs cannot deliver. Only through determined and consistent self-examination through cycles of death and rebirth is character intentionally formed. The method by which you forge character, the framework, is the same for endeavors of any kind. Human achievement and change are accomplished by a clear vision followed by decisive action(s) taken after sound decisions and supported by necessary resources. This framework is captured in the Military Decision-Making Process (MDMP) and outlined by Dallas Willard as "Vision-Intention-Means." Roll up your sleeves.

As my military career ramped up and our nation went to war, Mama Kay asked me why I wouldn't choose an easier line of work. "One day you'll be old", she said. "If you beat up your body your whole life it will be hard for you when you're old. Don't you want to take care of yourself?" Any second-year psychology student could unpack that statement disguised as a question and find a host of things to be curious about. I did not. I answered, "No. I want to use myself up and see how much a body can take. When I die, I want to leave a marred corpse to bury, covered in scars, dust, and partially healed wounds." Scars tell our stories for us.

Ships in harbors gather barnacles. Our bodies, minds, and hearts were given to us to use. Miraculously, the harder I try to wear them out, the stronger they get. We're designed that way. The human system of systems responds to challenges and stressors through adaptation and growth. Going easy on ourselves is what slowly kills us.

Orthopraxy. What do Olde Tyme Strongmen and Stoic Philosophers have in common? *Orthopraxy.* Better philosophy is learned in the boxing ring than in the classroom. In short, orthodoxy is "correct belief." Orthopraxy is "correct conduct." Misalignment between orthodoxy and orthopraxy is at the heart of many religious scandals. Strongmen, boxers, and Stoics do not care much about what someone else purports to believe. Actions are descendants of beliefs and, as such, provide significantly better markers than words.

They care a great deal about what beliefs look like in action, because actions are the truest proof of what someone *really* believes. They want to know what is *effective*. The only reliable method to determine effectiveness is through action. If I say, "I believe _____", the necessary question is "What does that look like in action?" Virtues in motion are recognizable: justice, humility, honesty, discipline, and courage. Let's say I believe I'm a good father. Prove it. Precisely, what it is that I consistently *do* that validates my belief? Beliefs without action do not change people. Conversely, if I claim to believe something but do not, sooner or later my actions will reflect my true belief(s). Like the value of the U.S. dollar when backed by reserve gold, the Gold Standard of old, words are valued by the actions that back them.

Like the U.S. dollar of today, printed at whim and value-manipulated through economic mechanisms, I can print words all day and spray the world with them. Without action, they're meaningless. A classic example is the jerk in an abusive relationship. He acts out, hurts people, and then apologizes. He tries to make up for it by being nice. Then he hits the repeat button, and the cycle continues. It does not take long for a rational person to recognize that his apologies are meaningless.

Most scenarios in our lives are less dire. My spouse asks me for the hundredth time to please not leave my wet towel on the floor. I tell her, "I'll try to do better about that." The next day, I leave my wet towel on the floor. One day, she murders me in my sleep. If you catch yourself saying that you'll try to do better about something, stop yourself. Stop talking. You are either going to do it or you are not going to do it. Commit to one or the other. Yoda said it. There is no "try." Do or do not do. Switching roles, if my spouse tells me honestly that she will never pick up her wet towel, I can work with that. I am then free to decide if I can live with a wet towel on the floor, if I am willing to pick it up every day for the rest of my life, or if this is the hill that I will die on. How much does it matter? Evaluate, decide, and act. I can either let it go or decide that it's a deal breaker. "I'll try to do better about that" traps us in a cycle of disappointment, resentment, and passive aggression. It's a lie. Honesty breaks the cycle.

Evaluate yourself. Know. Decide. Act.

When I was 13 years old, I started doing pull-ups, sit-ups, and push-ups in the unfinished basement of our family home. Big Bob had installed a rickety calisthenics system designed for a doorway in the middle of the basement. It had an adjustable sit-up board, a pull-up bar, and padded elbow arms where you could perform "Roman Chairs", a circa 1985 six-pack abs exercise. I knew nothing about training, except what I'd seen in the movie *Rocky*. It is not clear to me when the seed was planted or why I so clearly envisioned a stronger, better me at that age. I've psychoanalyzed my young self and suspect several variables. Regardless of my motivations,

I trained on my own every night before bed, almost seven days a week, for over two years. With no framework for effective training, I simply attempted to add one repetition (rep) to each exercise every day. As young as I was, I could recover quickly from bodyweight exercise, so it was not an ineffective way to start. Over time, I began to miss the additional rep or it would take longer to add a rep. But, by the time I turned 14, about 9 months later, I could do 40+ pull-ups without stopping, 147 push-ups in a row, and so many sit-ups that I timed them instead of counting them, e.g., as many as possible in ten minutes. My only goal was to add one rep to a single set every day for as long as I could. Once I couldn't add reps, I started doing multiple sets. The next school year, I looked different and had more confidence. I was better at football and skateboarding. People noticed. I was still a skinny, shy, and awkward teenage boy, but I had a growing sense of a secret power. Training alone in my basement gave me a psychological edge. I felt quietly *capable*. I didn't tell anyone that I worked out. I kept it to myself. That pivotal experience taught me several lessons I've not forgotten.

- First, the benefits of physical fitness extend far beyond your body and contribute to cognitive, psychological, and emotional stability.
- Second, working on myself without encouragement and in "secret" gave me a psychological edge. The Sage advised us to tithe and to pray in secret, where only the Father is witness, promising a greater reward. "Don't let your left hand know what your right hand is doing." Those who trumpet their good deeds have received their reward. The momentary approval of others is all that they get. There is much more for those willing to wait.
- Third, I never need a bunch of fancy equipment or ideal conditions to make positive changes. I use what I have on hand and don't delay. It's never the "right" time.
- Fourth, even when there is an overwhelming volume of things that need work, I can always strive to add one good rep to my capacity. Add one rep every day and your seventh-grade year looks a lot different than your sixth-grade year. I can always get one rep better than yesterday: one rep stronger, one rep more patient, one rep kinder, one rep more educated, one rep more

useful, one rep wiser. It is never too early or too late to start.

Self-Mastery. A common characteristic of masters across domains is their singular understanding of worlds within worlds. Within the boundaries of a master's small slice of life, they uncover in their specialties virtual galaxies of interwoven life – the musician in a simple instrument of six strings, the chef in common ingredients we might find in our kitchens at home, the psychologist in her run-of-the-mill clients, and the craftsman in his wood. Imagine the chef or cooky grandmother who first assembled the ingredients for what we now know as pizza. Mind-blowing.

What if I could find the same inspiration or experience the same profound beauty by losing myself in the menial tasks that I perform during any given day? What if it isn't the creation of the artistic mind or the scientific discovery, i.e., the products themselves, that are the gateway to the master's experience, but the close, focused, and full experience of a thing, the symphonic movements of a mechanism, the long-term result of paying close attention, the payoff from full cognitive, bodily, and spiritual investment? It is worth considering that such investment into any worthwhile action may open the path to a richer life. At levels of mastery, when done repeatedly over long periods, the commonplace offers moments of mystical enlightenment. Ordinary is extraordinary. Many things that I take for granted appear commonplace because I do not understand them. In today's Western world, what we need is not more scope but more depth. Learn to do what you are doing and nothing else.

Don't set lofty goals. Instead, determine paths, trajectories, or lines of effort. A goal is simply the next clearly defined action you will take. Define success not by the imagined end state but by consistent and well-executed effort along the path. Compare yourself to yourself yesterday, not yourself to a future ideal. Recognize and appreciate progress. When you keep promises to yourself, tell yourself, "Good job. Keep it up. Get back to work." That's the extent of the celebration.

Acknowledge progress, feel good about it, and drive on. Determine a program that is designed to yield the results you want and immerse yourself in each rep. Along the way, systematically take stock of the results over time. Adjust. Keep going. Be patient. Don't try to lose 30 pounds in 30 days. Stop eating sugar and see what happens in 30 days. Take stock. Make more adjustments. Keep going. Don't add 100 pounds to your back squat in eight weeks. Add 5 pounds every week. In a year, if you're built for it and all supporting variables are active, you'd add 260 pounds. Read 15 pages each day and, on average, you'll read about 25 books every year. Get up 30 minutes earlier every day and you'll add 10,950 minutes to your year, 182.5 hours, or 7.6 days (I'm not a mathematist. Feel free to double-check my calculations. The point abides). That's "free" time. All you must do is claim it. In a lifespan of 75 years, that 30 minutes adds up to an extra 1.56 *years*. Little things add up. Little things done consistently are big things.

A good place to start is by making two lists. One list is things you'd like to start doing that you know are beneficial to you and to those around you. An easy start is with chores or projects that have piled up. If you don't know what else to do, clean out your garage or organize your office. Detail your car. Go through your closet and donate things you never wear. Addressing your external physical life is a gateway to addressing your internal life. The second list is things that are not healthy for you, bad habits, things that keep coming up that you know aren't in your best interest or the interest of those around you.

This is not depth psychology. Wisdom begins with a grasp of the obvious. We all have ripe fruit to pick from the tree of life and obvious weeds growing in our yards. Pick some fruit and pull some weeds. Keep it simple. Prioritize. Pick one thing to start and one thing to stop. Apply the Pareto Principle to your choices, on the upside and downside. What's the biggest bang for your buck? Is there a thing that, if you started it, would benefit 80% of your life? Is there one thing that if you stopped would reduce 80% of your problems? Addictions are obvious examples. Simply start or stop the one thing that will make the most difference overall.

This is easy to write. It is not always easy to do. The One Thing might be a doozy. It may take a complete overhaul of your life to accomplish it. If so, get practice first with smaller things. Get a few wins under your belt. Experience the feeling of making headway. Work up to the big thing if necessary. If the big thing keeps you from making progress elsewhere, you have no choice but to square up to it, no matter what it takes. Face the thing that scares you the most. Avoidance is slow-motion suicide.

On habits. Success is a habit. Aristotle said, "We are what we repeatedly do. Excellence is not an act but a habit." Mediocrity is also a habit. Growing healthier is the result of a constellation of mutually supporting habits. A constellation of self-defeating habits results in continued and worsening dysfunction and sickness. If I don't like what I'm getting, I must change what I'm doing.

There must exist a reliable system. If there's no system, create one. A system yields results consistent with its design. If results are unfavorable, identify and adjust causative variables in the system to create a desired outcome. Your life is a system of systems, just as your body is. You have a system of personal hygiene, another for feeding, and another to socialize or pursue hobbies. Earning income is a system of systems all its own. Understanding the systems at play in your life enables you to alter them to create different outputs.

From the back cover of *The Power of Habit*, "Duhigg presents a whole new understanding of human nature and potential. ... The key to exercising regularly, losing weight, being more productive, and achieving success is understanding how habits work." Habits function according to a model of "Cue-Routine (Action)-Reward." Outside the context of the studies and scientific findings explained in the book, the model appears oversimplified. This is not the case. It is elegant. Instead of creating "new" habits, which takes time and neurological adaptation, you can convert old habits into new ones. It's a two-for-one deal! Two of Duhigg's most illuminating findings explained the roles of willpower and self-discipline. Self-discipline enables the exertion of willpower toward the creation or recreation of habits. Children who exhibit self-control and self-discipline outperform children who don't across every metric. Once behavior is habitualized, it becomes automatic, whether creative or destructive. That's why people who consistently "do well" make it look easy, children included. When the overwhelming bulk of a person's habits are healthy and productive, that is the tenor of their lives, their baseline normal, and their rhythmic flow. Once the beat is set you move to the rhythm.

Addictions have physical and psychological elements. The most dangerous of them to break have significant physical ramifications. All require psychological "treatment" of some kind, whether professional or otherwise. Thoughts drive feelings. Feelings engender thoughts. The thought-feeling cycle drives actions. Repeated actions create physical addictions. Hedonic adaptation ensures that you will require more and more input for fewer rewards. You must get your head right to kick addictions.

Emotional "addictions" are bad habits. Bad habits won't kill you if you stop. Some things you can simply stop. If I have a habit of blaming others for my failings, I can choose to stop. Many emotional bad habits feel good. Anger feels good. Self-pity feels good. Acting like a toddler can be fun, albeit unbecoming. The onset of such emotions is natural, but continuing in them intentionally is self-indulgence, not emotion. It's a form of immaturity and is selfish. Self-indulgence is often at the root of many dysfunctional habits. Gossip is one example. Taking the last brownie is another. Decide that you don't want to be "that person" and knock it off.

On Grit. I learned more useful life skills by putting myself through college than I did in college classrooms. I was the first college graduate that I know of on either side of my family. It took me five years to graduate with a four-year degree. I started my freshman year with a new, pregnant wife (high school girlfriend), two jobs, and student loans to pay tuition. My wife was also enrolled, studying to become a nurse. We had to coordinate our class schedules and sometimes swap our daughter in between. There were days (at least one I clearly remember) when she waited for me in the Student Union building with our daughter while I went to class.

Once I'd finished my class, I'd hustle to the Union and sit with the baby so that she could go to her class. She shouldered the bulk of the challenge as a single mother because of our custody arrangement. We divorced after a year but kept at it. She graduated and finished nursing school. I graduated and joined the Marines. I learned a lot in college and value my education. Even as an English literature major with a creative writing emphasis, which does not appear particularly relevant to most careers, learning how to read books, extract information, and communicate effectively improved my performance in every professional role that followed.

The relentless challenge of juggling responsibilities as a father, earning enough to support myself, and completing coursework taught me how to endure. I got gritty. A good friend of mine, call sign Night Clerk, attended the U.S. Naval Academy as a football player. He attended a preparatory year followed by four years at the Academy. At least one summer, he had to attend make-up courses for a low grade in a particularly tough class. Of his experience, he taught me that it is not always the smartest or most talented who can survive the rigorous classwork and the demands of college football.

Most often, it is the student who refuses to give up. He said something to the effect that, "If you endure long enough, one day you're the last man standing." Do what it takes. If it's important, sacrifice for it. Treat your life like you're on a football team and stay after practice to run extra sprints, then stay up all night studying. Earn the hard yards. Don't stop until you hear the whistle. Hold fast. Get gritty.

A high school friend of mine, who later became a rabid entrepreneur, once told me, "I don't burn bridges, I blow them up." He was not referring to relationships, but safety nets. He was a "burn the boats" thinker. Safety nets can provide the confidence of a solid backup plan or a financial cushion. They can also short-circuit total commitment. Our greatest and sometimes only chance of success is to go all in. Contingency plans that maintain forward progress are superior to those that take me back to where I was.

The Integration of Your Shadow. Shadow integration is the process of making oneself whole. It is psychological in origin but involves and requires involvement from our bodies and feeling centers. In spiritual or religious traditions, this integration or re-integration is known as the "restoration of the soul", with the soul as the center for executive processing in my being. For my understanding of shadow integration and the path down which it has led me, I am, again, indebted to Robert A. Johnson. *Owning Your Own Shadow* was the first of his books that I found and many since have opened a deeper understanding of our human plight and my struggles. I've read it numerous times.

Johnson depicts, through analogous story and myth-telling, the deepest truths of human experience. Our deepest psychologies touch our most ancient spiritualities. In the discussion that follows, excerpts from my notes capture the ideas most profound in my journey. Any failures to accurately quote Johnson or errors in interpretation are mine. I am not a psychologist. If you are curious, go to the source. Read his book(s).

My shadow is comprised of repressed, undeveloped, un-actuated, or inferior function(s). These are not necessarily to be equated with our "dark side." They are not evil by virtue of existing in the shadow, nor are the fully expressed functions of our ego necessarily good. It is not a good versus evil dynamic. During the inculturation process growing up, we develop our ego. Our ego is a necessary mechanism of aggregated functions. Societies function on tacit social contracts of behavior. We learn what is acceptable and what is not. Acceptance is a social reward. Rewards teach us how to present ourselves to the world so that we are better able to survive and thrive. The ego is what we construct to represent who we "are." I think of my ego as my persona or identity. It is sometimes called the "false self." Adaptability is a learned skill to activate elements of our ego appropriately within specific contexts. The function least accepted or effective is relegated to our shadow.

A benign but profound example was my transition from college to military service. I studied English literature, poetry, saxophone, French, and creative writing. Success in college required immersion in artistic endeavor. Creativity and uniqueness were valued. I fully embraced the persona of a long-haired, mild-mannered wordsmith and bookworm with a certain sartorial flair. Then I joined the U.S. Marine Corps. The *Gun Club* was a different egoic planet than the humanities side of a college campus.

Adapting to that environment required the subjugation of well-honed functions in favor of those valued in a different context. Being critical and creative took a back seat to obedience, physical toughness, assertiveness, and conformity. I was once ordered to report to my commander to discuss an infraction. Standing at parade rest in front of his desk, he handed me a piece of paper. On it, I had completed a handwritten course critique. "What's wrong with this," asked the Commander. I scanned for misspellings, grammatical errors, and unprofessional content. To me, it appeared to be a well-written and thoughtful response to the feedback questions. The infraction I had committed was using a pen with blue ink. "We don't use blue ink in the Marine Corps, lieutenant." Roger that. Note to ego.

Our shadows contain much of our power. Johnson asserts that shadow functions are often our most noble capacities, what he refers to as our "gold." We are more frightened of our nobility than of our lesser capacities. Being dysfunctional, or not fully optimized, lets me off the hook because I am not responsible for doing what I "cannot" do. But we are capable of more than we realize or will admit. Johnson says that the cultured individual with an equally strong shadow has great power. With power comes responsibility. I may desire more power but shy from increased responsibility.

To avoid my most noble self is to deny myself access to many of the most brilliant and powerful energies that reside within. Johnson said, "Heaven for form and Hell for energy." Religion means "to bind again." In our exploration of ourselves and our lives best lived, we must "get religion." We must make room for all our elements. We must become aware of the faculties in us that we have ignored and make space for expression. The S-shaped line through the middle of the Yin and Yang symbol represents The Way.

Walking The Way requires one foot in the known and one in the unknown. The Way represents symmetry and balance. It recruits stability and confidence from the known parts of our lives and infuses life with the energy and creativity of the unknown. Johnson takes care to point out that not all integration requires the *literal* expression of undeveloped functions. Acknowledgment and ritual create space where long-ignored energies can be honored and integrated without upheaval. Johnson offers a practical framework to assess the clashing of the Ego and our shadows.

Competing energies seem to contradict each other. There is internal conflict. Egoic development is a process of compartmentalization, seeking to shelf certain capacities in favor of others and to minimize internal conflict. Contradiction is destructive. Johnson points out that from contrast, however, comes paradox. Paradox captures the most sublime principles of human experience. You must lose your life to find it; less is more; discipline is freedom; the last shall be first; when you give you receive; and if you humble yourself, you will be lifted.

Meditation is not what you think. Choose what's hard and life is easier but choose what's easy and life gets harder. You must get out of your head to discover what's in it. To say "yes" to life, you must learn to say "no" to yourself. Johnson describes the richness of contrast, e.g., the contrast of flavors and textures to create a sublime dining experience. Sometimes all that is needed is a mental shift from perceiving contradiction to perceiving contrast. Instead of judging that "these conflict", simply observe that "these are not the same." Contrasts create depth and add dimension. In contrast with another, one thing is more fully known and seen. Contrast creates beauty and unexpected delight. Johnson says that the capacity for integrated paradox is the measure of spiritual strength and maturity. It is the hallmark of the enlightened.

When our ego is fully exploited and our known capacities worn out, our shadows provide a new lease on life. Correctly handled, this hinge period can be a time of growth. Stupidly or carelessly handled, it can lead to the loss of form and structure, implosion, and even destruction. Johnson, quoting Carl Jung, said, "Heaven and skid row are separated only by an act of consciousness." Kierkegaard said, "Purity of heart is to will one thing." Johnson explains that Eastern mystics consider the Mind of God to be One Mind.

Indecision is the result of a fragmented mind out of alignment with the Source. The intentional synthesis of our capacities aligned with a higher purpose illuminates The Way. It binds us together and binds us to God, the Great Spirit, the Universe, or the Common Good. Shadow integration trades mutually exclusive compromises for unification. The Single Eye of great mystical traditions is the unification of disparate human elements into a single purpose fueled with power and love. Stockdale said that the heart is the only repository for things of absolute value.

Find the Mystical in the Mundane. I become what I continually fill myself with. My worldview is created by the thoughts that I grind repeatedly in my mind, like a cow chewing cud. If they are negative, my outlook is such. Complaints, I am dissatisfied. Injustices and blame, I am a victim. Edifying, I am filled with goodwill.

I can't give away what I don't have. I must possess what I profess, as George Fox, founder of the Quakers, put it. I can pretend to be something that I am not, but I cannot transfer it. An author named Charles Chamberlain used a metaphor. I'm an empty dirty glass. I begin to fill myself with clear, clean water. Slowly, my glass fills and my glass gets cleaner. Eventually, I overflow and can pour into the lives of others. But stagnant water turns sour and sick. The stream must pour in, and I must pour out.

This is the concept of "being." I become what I fill myself with. What I "am" is what I can give freely to others. Bumper stickers, sweatshirts, and coffee mugs encourage me to "just be" or "just breathe." Folding my legs and sitting in a self-righteous spiritual pose does not change me unless my spirit, mind, and body relinquish control. Going to church doesn't make me a good person any more than wandering around a gym makes me strong. When I sit in silence, recognizing my smallness and need for the Great Spirit, "being" becomes awareness of what I am – beautiful and ugly – and that I can be in this moment only that which I am. This doesn't acquit me. If I don't like what I see, the choice is mine to either accept it or pour new water into myself. I must act to change.

It is advisable to learn at a cellular level. Cellular-level learning requires a teachable spirit, a thoughtful mind, and a body in action. Whole-person activity synthesizes knowledge into being through bodily living. The most effective combination is the desperation of the dying with the inspiration of the spirit. Inspiration = fill with air. I need the oxygen of the spirit when I'm moving. "In Him [The Logos] I move and breathe and have my being." This is mind-body-spirit engaged in and focused on the task at hand.

When The Sage said the Kingdom of Heaven is at hand, I do not believe that only means that heaven is here but I can't see it. I believe also that heaven is the ability to see what is right here, right now, as all that there is. It's all that ever is. It's all that we ever have and it is heavenly when infused with divine senses. When I find myself practicing The Principles on the task at hand, engrossed in it with all five senses, it becomes beautiful, connected, necessary, and worthwhile. I experience the assurance that I am fortunate to be doing it.

I glimpse heaven. When I'm doing the thing without thought of being elsewhere, my spirit seeking guidance, my mind at full processing speed, and my body getting it done, my cells quicken and my neurons fire new paths. I am becoming. I do one thing – one rep – fully and everything changes. I've done many things. Those are already done. There is more to do. We'll get to that later. Do this first, just this. That's where it begins and that's where it ends. That's all there is to it.

Get Your Hands Dirty. I've had a lot of jobs, from menial to manual to deskwork. It's made me a cross-functional generalist, a master of none. Midway through my career, I discovered somewhere a concept called the "90-Day Burn." Each time I start a new job or begin a new learning cycle, I fence the first 90 days and block time for total immersion and myopic focus. It includes learning everything I can about the job, meeting as many people as I can and learning from them, researching secondary and tertiary resources to establish a context in scope, and getting my boots on the ground and my hands in the mix from the bottom up. In positions of leadership, it is particularly vital to understand what the tasks and a routine workday look like for the foundational echelon of the organization.

General Mattis said, "Listen, learn, help, then lead." Spending time on the ground equips me with information and experience vital to decision-making. More importantly, it carves out time to get to know people. The pinnacle of effective leadership is relational, not positional. Influence and collaboration trump authority and command presence. On teams, round tables beat rectangular ones. As I've matured, the 90-Day Burn has evolved from an exercise in getting as productive as possible as quickly as possible to an opportunity to fully connect. In a system of systems, there are people, things, knowledge, and ideas. There are processes, precedents, and products. I seek first to connect with each of these to create a map. From the map, I can then make connections between people and things.

I understand the capacities of available resources. From a place of understanding, I can observe, diagnose, and be useful. Leadership becomes a fulfilling charge to appropriately provide resources and remove obstacles on behalf of a team that you know and love (or at least respect). If I am not the leader, the 90-Day Burn puts me in a better position to contribute to the overall success of the team and to "lead up", i.e., to anticipate problems and bring potential solutions to my boss. The 90-Day Burn is an effective method to get into anything. Whatever you want to get into, do it with your whole person. Experience and absorb as much as you can. Be curious. Be amazed. Become useful.

Speechless. My favorite professor in college, David Kranes, walked into class one day and, without speaking to the class, wrote on the chalkboard, "The best things in life cannot be told. The second best are misunderstood. Then comes civilized conversation, then mass indoctrination, then intercultural exchange." -Joseph Campbell

We understand the deepest human truths in a way that we cannot articulate. Timeless stories indirectly capture truths or morals. The truth cannot be "told", but it can be depicted in a way that we *know* it. Possibly the shortest story ever written, attributed variously to different authors, is a notional newspaper classified ad. "For sale: baby shoes, never worn." Six words that point toward a world within a world, a narrative of hope, desperation, and devastation that we write in our minds.

The reader is the author of this story. We are always the readers and authors of stories. Experience is a story that we write. The deeper our experiences, the richer our narratives. The first requirement for deep experience is presence. The most direct method to be present during an experience is to recruit all five of your senses, and possibly a sixth, instead of one or two. Try it with your next meal. Slow down and eat each bite. See the colors, listen to the sounds around you and the sound your fork makes on the plate, smell each bite before you take it, feel the texture of the food and the heat rising from your plate, and taste the contrasts of flavors. Or try it in your next face-to-face conversation.

Listen not only to words but to tones, observe facial expressions, watch their eyes, and note how their mouth forms words. Look for tension or relaxation in their shoulders, breathe deeply, and touch a hand or an arm while you talk. Paying attention to what is happening is the first step toward discovering what it means to live your life, the actual life you are currently living. I read in one of Robert Johnson's books, that *happiness* and *happening* have the same root word. Happiness is a derivative of happening, happiness being that state of excitement about, contentment with, or acceptance of what is happening. In moments of full connection, I realize that I don't need a new life. The one I have is so complex and fascinating that I'd need an eon to discover it all. I simply need to pay more attention.

Breathe Behind the Shield. Pavel Tsatsouline in *The Naked Warrior*, as well as *Simple and Sinister* and other writings, underscores the imperative of what Bruce Lee called "breath strength." Controlled power breathing and intraabdominal pressure (IAP) correlate directly to muscular strength. The point is to create abdominal pressure by contracting your diaphragm, pushing your organs toward your belly, and creating compression. "Never inhale or exhale all the way." The ideal volume of air in your body is about 75%. One of Pavel's techniques to achieve this is the Iron Shirt. It's a "bottom-up" method that starts with an anal lock. Check it out!

During a punch or lift, a small amount of air escapes in the form of a grunt or hiss. Following the punch or rep, a gulp of fresh air replaces it. It isn't breathing as we commonly think about it. It's pressure control. The compression in your abdomen forms a balloon of energy. You can punch harder and you can lift more. An added benefit – a primary benefit when it gets heavy – is safety. Pavel also calls breath strength "breathing behind the shield." It "enables high trunk stability, typically associated with breath holding, while keeping the oxygen flowing."

A compressed abdomen creates a layer of protection from inbound kicks and maximal weightlifting or heavy kettlebell swings. Done correctly, you can lay on your back, compress your abdomen with breath, and have someone stand on your stomach. No problem. Breathing behind the shield makes you stronger and protects you from injury. Regrettably, it is rarely discussed in Western fitness protocols outside specialty disciplines like powerlifting and martial arts.

Martial arts masters have said that breath strength is fundamental to their practice. Without it, there is no strength. The art becomes a form lacking power. Much like "beach muscles", it appears to be something it is not. Country music legend Waylon Jennings sang, "It ain't how you look, it's what you got under the hood." The Bible denounces those who have a "form of Godliness" but deny the power. They miss the point. Breath is life. The ancient Greek word for *breath* was *pneuma*. In Greek tragedies, it translated as "breath of life." Translated throughout the New Testament, it is used for *spirit*. Breath is spirit. Breath is Spirit. Giving up the ghost, or spirit, is breathing your last.

Breath is being. I use breathing behind the shield as a euphemism to remind myself that dedication to becoming better is not a matter of appearance, neither physically nor in persona. It is not egoic. It has nothing to do with the view others have of me. It is internal. At cellular and systemic levels, I seek to tap into what nature freely offers. Rooted, or centered, in Marcus Aurelius' "inner citadel", I align my purpose with the collective good or the Great Spirit. Nature invites us to live according to its "laws" and provides free of charge the breath of life necessary to fuel such a life. Without it, my flailings and floggings are trivial and pointless machinations.

Devoid of centered purpose, my attempts to appear that I have it all together are a form lacking function. They garner one-dimensional rewards. Anchored depth powers meaningful exchange and functional strength across domains. It's the pressure control of life in the spirit. Breathe behind the shield.

Train Like You Fight. Our bodies are not geometric. We are not sketched using straight lines, right angles, or with a calculable hypotenuse. The limitations of Nautilus machines, hip sleds, and a Smith rack are that they force our bodies to attempt the replication of natural motion but restrict movement to straight lines. They may have their place in a well-planned program but are inherently inadequate in the context of transference to real-life functions. This is relevant in degrees. If my intention for building functional capacity in the gym is to make me better at doing things outside the gym, it stands to reason that I'd choose movements directly transferable.

To maximize the effectiveness, I must train like I live. Hence, "sport-specific" training versus "General Physical Preparedness" as frameworks toward utility. In military training, replicating the conditions of the battlefield or a specific scenario as closely as possible better prepares you for the real thing. Tier One units have been known to use intelligence to reconstruct entire buildings in which to train, so that when they hit the target they've "been there before." The realism of training is directly proportional to the speed at which a trainee can adapt to real-world conditions. The human mind and body are so adaptable that a well-trained soldier can almost feel at home in the direst conditions. This sense of having been in a chaotic, dangerous scenario before equates to systemic stability, a clear(er) head, functional capacity, and survivability.

For some things, replication is always incomplete as a tool for preparation. To get good at the thing you must do the thing. Long-distance running is an example. A medic responding to a horrible vehicle accident is another. Combat certainly is. A boxer's first fight. The best-trained athletes, first responders, and soldiers are inevitably met with surprises during their first race, first patient, or first gunfight.

However, there are predictable elements that can be incorporated into training so that surprises are anomalies instead of a cascade of overwhelming inputs and stimulations. As you map lines of effort across functional areas, practice things the way you want to do them and in the conditions your capabilities are most likely to be needed. If no one has told you today, you have a great hypotenuse! Build a plan based on reality.

How to Read a Book. In the 1940s, college was hard. A shift in societal thinking from exclusion to inclusion, including the idea that a college education is a "right" for every citizen, necessarily forced academic institutions first to lower entrance standards and then soften the rigors of curricula. Regardless of quibbles on either side of the argument, allowing *everyone* into college required that it be easy enough that *everyone* stood a chance of graduating. I both benefitted and paid the price for that. My college experience was not overly challenging. Had it been tougher, I may not have graduated. However, had it been tougher I may have risen to the challenge and graduated a better-equipped thinker and doer.

I'll never know. William A. Henry III, in his book *In Defense of Elitism*, describes the university experience of his mother. Despite having only three career choices, secretary, nurse, or schoolteacher, the scholastic rigors of her curriculum were no different from any other student. She was required to earn a "classical" education. That meant that she didn't sample Shakespeare, she read everything he'd ever written in a single semester and was required to produce critical essays showcasing her ability to think. She had to learn Latin and one other foreign language. She had to be conversant in math, science, and the humanities.

A college graduate was expected to be conversant on a broad range of topics, to display powers of critical thinking, to express informed opinions, and to express an understanding of the human experience within the context of two millennia of collective knowledge. The dynamic between students and professors was deliberately combative. Students were expected to think, formulate and defend arguments, and stand their ground in classroom debates against professors and other students. Shockingly, university students in the 1940s were not allowed to focus their studies on whatever they wanted without having first established a required baseline of universal knowledge, including *moral knowledge*.

Specializing was reserved for graduate work. Undergraduate students did not get to invent degrees nor were academic departments allowed to exist based on self-referential academic incest. Undergraduate rigors were designed so that students learned how to think, how to argue, and how to contribute based on a high standard of classical knowledge. Students performed or were expelled. As such, a bachelor's degree was highly valued. I graduated college in the 1990s.

There were only a few hard classes I was *required* to take. I read a lot of books, learned a little math and science, and enjoyed an elective class on Human Sexuality that turned out to be long on biology and short on techniques, which was disappointing. I did not learn Latin, logic, or debate. The value that I and potential employers placed on my diploma was commensurate with the effort required to earn it. What does a dude with a degree in English and a

"B" grade point average do? He joins the Gun Club. The Marines understood. They're good like that.

Inclusivity for its own sake requires the lowering of standards and results in the devaluation of the final product. This leads me to my point, fellow autodidacts. Since most generalized university studies alone will not prepare me for the intellectual demands of high function, I must learn how to read.

In the beginning of 1940, Mortimer J. Adler and Charles Van Doren published the first edition of their book, aptly titled *How to Read a Book*. In addition to providing significant insight into the theory of knowledge, the book dedicates some 421 pages to explaining the goals, dimensions, and four levels of reading, and provides different approaches tailored to different types of reading. The authors offer a prescient criticism of the role of media (all types) in the erosion of people's ability to think for themselves. Learning to read actively, intentionally, and intelligently is the antidote. Forming worthwhile opinions demands it. Being a bag of hot air does not.

> "Perhaps we know more about the world than we used to, and insofar as knowledge is a prerequisite to understanding, that is all to the good. But knowledge is not as much a prerequisite to understanding as is commonly supposed. We do not have to know everything about something in order to understand it; too many facts are often as much of an obstacle to understanding as too few. There is a sense in

which we moderns are inundated with facts to the detriment of understanding. One of the reasons for this situation is that the very media we have mentioned are so designed as to make thinking seem unnecessary (though this is only an appearance). The packaging of intellectual positions and views is one of the most active enterprises of some of the best minds of our day. ... [The viewer or listener] inserts a packaged opinion into his mind, somewhat like inserting a cassette into a cassette player. He then pushes a button and 'plays back' the opinion whenever it seems appropriate to do so. He has performed successfully without having to think."[20]

This was the State of the Nation less than a century ago. I suspect that the authors might underscore the above as more prevalent and perilous today than in human history. Thinking for yourself is more valuable now than ever. Thinking well requires that you learn to read well.

On Homework, side work, desk work, and wet work. "Finding your labor of love is almost always preceded by cultivating a love of labor." -Andrew Huberman

#goanalogorgohome. International travel has afforded me many experiences stripped of creature comforts. I realize how rarely I think of the many comforts I enjoy, and my lack of daily gratitude for them, when they are suddenly

---

[20] M. Adler, and C. Van Doren, *How to Read a Book* (New York: Simon & Schuster, 1972), 4.

unavailable. The Stoics practiced *futurorum malorum premeditatio*, or *premeditatio malorum*, which was the visualization of a worst-case scenario. The point was to imagine the worst possible outcome and recognize that you could not only survive it but live well through it.

Some philosophers went as far as living it out for a prescribed period. If my fear was poverty, I might spend a week living as though I were destitute. From the temporary reality of destitution, I find that it's not nearly as bad as I had imagined. My fear is then alleviated and I can return to my life with greater gratitude. I can experience what's captured in an old Marine admonition – defiance in the face of adversity – where "every paycheck is a fortune and every meal is a feast", despite meager sums and Meals-Ready-to-Eat. Seneca said, "Who fears serves."

Another aspect of modern Western life is that it has insulated us from discomfort of all kinds. I once needed a new lawnmower. Enamored by the nostalgic qualities (and the price) of a version with no motor, the base model cylinder of shears on two wheels, I embarked on a lawn maintenance journey that was illuminating. The machine is simple. As you push it, the blades spin with the wheels and shear the grass blades much as scissors. The shearing leaves a healthier and aesthetically pleasing blade end for detailed work on grass, such as golfing greens. For turning long grass into short grass on your front lawn, the push mower is a workout. I quickly discovered that I had to put my back into it. After a couple of mows, I learned that push mowers must be kept clean, free of debris, well-oiled, and blades sharpened. Mowing is work and maintenance is required.

Despite the inconvenience, I stuck with it. Its simplicity was elegant. After a single inspection, I understood how the machine worked and how to maintain it. It never requires fuel, spark plugs, or filters. The spinning blades reflected sunlight and the blades rang a *shing-shing-shing* sound as the cylinder turned. After mowing, rinsing, drying, and oiling it became a ritual of completion and stewardship. It was light enough to hang on a sturdy wall hook in my garage.

There is intrinsic value in routinely stripping comforts, at least temporarily. Self-denial of any kind is self-validating. Try it to find out. Our bodies are fashioned to respond to discomfort and to adapt and grow. It is healthy to endure the elements of nature regularly. Be cold, be hot, sweat, shiver, and run until you're gasping for air. Turn off the air conditioner and open the windows. Do math in your head instead of on your phone's calculator. Train barefoot, outside, with no music. Mail someone a letter. Chop wood and build a fire. Sit by the fire and stare into it until you see your ancestors dancing. Hold your breath underwater. Live on rice and beans for a week. When the inventory system goes down, get a stubby pencil and a clipboard, Night Clerk style, and count the stuff the old-fashioned way. Get dirty. Call instead of text. Listen to a baseball game on the radio. Eat lunch on your tailgate. Get some sun. Eat the week-old leftover steak. Heat it on the stove instead of in the microwave. Go commando! Ride your bike instead of drive. And, the classic, take a cold shower.

Via Negativa. *Freedom* is the point (of self-improvement, psychotherapy, physical fitness, recovery, discipline, and meditation). These categories and any like them require that we pay a price. The price is immediate gratification. We must trade something now for something of greater value that we get later. We must learn to sacrifice and to wait. Fortitude is built by foregoing. A test designed for children assesses a child's ability to forego immediate gratification for the promise of a greater future reward. Sit a child at a table.

Set a cookie in front of them and offer them this choice: they can eat one cookie now, or they can have two cookies in 10 minutes. Let them know that neither choice is wrong or right and that it's entirely up to them to choose. Answer any clarifying questions they have. Set a timer for 10 minutes so that they can watch it count down. Tell the child you'll be back in a few minutes and leave them alone with the cookie. The choice to eat it now or wait is a tough one for a little kid and ten minutes is an eternity. A child's ability to consider his or her future self and to willingly engage in self-denial now in exchange for greater reward later is a determinant factor in the likelihood of future success. As we mature, the choice remains the same.

Remember (or look up) the Sucker's Folly. Self-denial has intrinsic value. Learning to tell ourselves "No" frees us from ourselves. I am my worst problem. Our lizard brains and our untended habits create insistent demands that we make of ourselves. The voices are loud. Neglect is endorsement. The tethers of addiction, comfort, medication, excessive grooming, materialism, self-obsession, distraction, and all manner of insidious self-conditioning and self-sabotage bind us. The Way of Via Negativa cuts one rope at a time.

I encountered the concept of Via Negativa first in the anthology Less is More. Later, Nassim Nicholas Taleb's Antifragile introduced me to sets and subsets of Via Negativa in application toward the end of antifragility. Taleb explains that *action* is often considered a thing while *inaction* is not, but he challenges the veracity of that logic. Inaction is also a thing. I thought of a black-and-white still-life photo in development. Regarding shapes and spaces, the artistic composition is the contrast of objects and non-objects, i.e., the spaces empty of objects include content, even that identified by conspicuous absence, and form shape. The quality of *not-being-an-object* has substance. The objects are identifiable because of their contrast with non-object space, not despite it.

Abstract art consists of the shapes and content of substance and space, occupied/unoccupied, presence/lack, each expressing the power that is its own. By this logic, non-action is as much a thing as action. Apt restraint of power exerts power. Meekness is the restraint of power, not the lack of power. The meek will inherit the earth. Deliberate non-action is sometimes the solution to a problem set, while action exacerbates the problem. In response to wildland forest fires, ecologists have learned that letting it burn is the best overall course of action. Containing a wildfire to prevent the consumption of homes is advisable, but the entire ecosystem relies on the natural cycle of destruction by fire, the recycling of elements into the earth, and regrowth. Except for the protection of human life and property, the best thing to do with a wildfire is nothing. Inaction is the appropriate action.

Observe this logic in the world of nutrition. If 50% of my diet consists of sugar and simple starches, I cannot add enough vitamins and exercise to ameliorate the negative results of my diet. If I were to stop eating sugar altogether, simply subtract a single thing from the equation, 80% of the problem is solved by what I *don't* do and without adding anything. To build muscle an athlete must do something (eat enough protein). To lose weight you must not do something (don't eat fructose/sucrose). On a Huberman Labs podcast, guest Dr. Robert Lustig offered essential information for understanding nutrition.

I'll paraphrase a few vital points. First, fructose is as addictive as heroin and there are no human biological or neurological processes that *require* fructose. We don't need it. Second, our bodies do not process food mathematically, i.e., the "calories in/calories out" argument for weight management, where I can run longer on the treadmill to burn off my dessert. It doesn't work that way. *What we eat is more important than how much.* I tend to think of my body more as a chemistry laboratory than a steel factory. The food I eat reacts and the reactions create effects. As such, the causation/correlation effects of the calories I consume are not directly related to the calories I burn.

Third, Dr. Lustig said that the "longevity tax" on chronic fructose consumption is 8-20 years. It slowly kills you. He also said that the Glycemic Index is bunk. Switch from thinking about a "low-carb" diet to a low-insulin diet, or low inflammation diet. Our bodies treat high levels of "blood sugar" with insulin. Chronically high insulin causes chronic inflammation and insulin stores excess glucose in fat. In short, Dr. Lustig said that humans can safely consume 7-10% of their calories in fructose, that highly processed food is definitively not food, and that fasting followed by fermented foods is good for your gut. Abs are made in the kitchen.

In my lifetime, the topic of sex education in public middle schools has been debated. Politics and religion notwithstanding, the problems of sexually transmitted diseases, unwanted pregnancy, and social degradation are solved by abstinence. Of course, this is true at any age. One mustn't forget that abstinence is an available option. Before releasing young Marines and soldiers for the weekend, Commanders and First Sergeants give the unit a "safety brief." It's a simple reminder to honor the code, i.e., stay out of trouble, while they're off base without supervision. Though content varies, two staples are, "If you drink, don't drive" and "If you have sex, wear protection."

The simplest (and least popular) solution to the risks of drunk driving or casual sex is to not do a specific thing. Attendant risk-mitigation efforts to prevent complications are irrelevant without the antecedent action. Marines and soldiers who don't drink alcohol and don't hook up with local girls tend to get themselves into less trouble overall than those who do and sober drivers don't get DUIs. I've never met a soldier who caught an STD by *not* having sex with someone. Those who engage in both simultaneously are gamblers.

Taleb argues that the same applies when it comes to knowledge, what he terms "subtractive epistemology." Summarized, "since one small observation can disprove a statement, while millions can hardly confirm it, disconfirmation is more rigorous than confirmation."[21] Avoiding ignorance wields power equal to that of cultivating wisdom. Talib quotes Steve Jobs, "People think focus means saying yes to the thing you've got to focus on. But that's not what it means at all. It means saying no to the hundred other good ideas that there are. You have to pick carefully. I'm actually as proud of the things we haven't done as the things I have done. Innovation is saying no to 1,000 things."[22]

On the Less is More front, Via Negativa applies broadly and is simple to implement. An old parable illustrates how it is applied in problem-solving (and therapy) by using the simplest means possible (and the evident principle of self-responsibility). When a barefoot traveler is confronted with a long and rocky path, she has two choices: 1) cover the entire world in leather, or 2) make herself a pair of sandals. Another maxim encourages us to make ourselves less easily offended instead of crusading to make the world less offensive. Elimination is a powerful principle.

[21] N. N. Taleb, *Antigragile: Things That Gain from Disorder* (New York: Random House, 2014), 303.
[22] Ibid., 305.

Externally, all around us are the piled, stored, and dusty reminders of our excess.

We already use only a fraction of the gadgets we own and repeatedly wear only a handful of our trusted favorites from our closets. How many coffee mugs and t-shirts does one man need? The elimination of superfluous objects from our lives is a great place to start. With a little practice, we can move to more difficult items and intangibles.

There is a correlation between fear and desire. Seneca said, "I would rather beg of myself not to desire a thing than beg of the Fates to bestow it upon me." Dallas Willard suggested that it is not the *elimination* of desire that is the goal but the *subordination* of desire to will—a will that is appropriately aligned with a Higher Will. Human desire is vital to life and the loss of it precludes a loss of zest for living. However, it is the will that is responsible for the governing of desire. Ungoverned, desire runs amok. Reference the evilest Roman emperors for examples.

For example, the reign of Marcus Aurelius, characterized by his personal commitment to virtue, is appallingly different than that of his son and heir, Commodus, who lived and ruled to satisfy his every desire. Commodus nearly annihilated in a few short years what five good emperors in succession, his father included, had built over the previous century. The unconscious alignment of our will to selfishness or intentional alignment with a higher purpose determines how we govern—or do not govern—our desires.

Practicing Via Negativa has a double benefit in the curbing of unconscious desire and the elimination of extracurricular fears. Most good is the absence of bad. Eliminating unhealthy or excessive elements from your life is the shortest route to health and the closest you can come to nature as it is intended. Detachment as a discipline is often misunderstood. Much of its treatment is found in mystical and deeply religious traditions. But it has deep philosophical roots also. Detachment is not the cultivation of aversion, but rather the cultivation of neutrality, what some might call acceptance. It is the Apostle Paul's admonition to "abase or abound" with equal gratitude and undisturbed peace. In therapeutic circles, my experience is that of separating external conditions from qualitative internal judgments.

Detachment means that I can "take it or leave it" with equivalent gratitude. The things I own don't own me. Things and people don't have their "hooks" in me. The chaos of the world, though I can keenly observe it, does not disrupt the quiet of my inner citadel. Desire is the gap between the way things are and the way I want them (or think they ought) to be. I actively practice not wanting things outside my control to be different than they are. I refrain from signing implicit contracts with myself that insist I cannot be happy until I get what I want. This takes practice. It is worth the effort.

By focusing on what is meaningful or necessary, and saying no to most else, I begin to have a clearer definition of "enough." Knowing how much is enough is a threshold on the path to freedom. Absent a defined or quantified satisfactory end state, there is never enough and there is never an end.

In his twenties, my uncle got a job at the local mill. He hated that job, mostly because he wasn't "cut out" for hard work, as he put it. Nonetheless, he worked that job for six years before he quit. Why six years? Once he had a steady paycheck, he bought a piece of land in the woods and put a double-wide trailer on it. He decided that if he were ever going to get free of "The Man" he'd have to own the trailer and land outright. It took him six years to pay it off. Once he owned it, he quit his job.

For the next forty or so years, he did odd jobs and spent his time in ways that suited him. He's not what most Americans would consider a success story. However, he had the clarity and the foresight, even through the haze of 1960's skunk weed, to *specifically define* what was *enough* for him. He submitted to the system exactly long enough to accomplish his goal and settle into the life he wanted. He lived his version of the American Dream without getting seduced by *more*.

The U.S. Government (USG) has a habit of adding programs but rarely discontinuing them. The greater the supply of funding the more numerous the programs (Parkinson's Law). Regardless of how the road to Hell is paved, once a program has outlived its purpose, continuation equates to "waste, fraud, and abuse", to describe it using the government's terminology. Nonetheless, government programs are systematically funded past their utility and well into their corruption, e.g., the FDA, FBI, IRS, and myriad others. This is not to say that these agencies aren't full of good, well-intentioned citizens. But government agencies themselves continue to exist long after their mission gets murky.

The murkier their purpose, the more bloated and populated they become. Default perpetuation is built into the system. It's more difficult to discontinue a program and reallocate resources than to simply write a check, until the day when there is too much month at the end of the money. Programs of this type exist to exist, mummify the status quo, defy economic imperatives, and create the ever-puzzling self-licking ice cream cone. How much is enough? When does it end? Defining this in your life is a fiscal imperative – no household can function like the USG – and it is more. Knowing how much is enough and what is unneeded is *spiritually* liberating and opens the path to generosity, fearlessness, and contentment.

Big Bob encapsulated the entire Bible and the foundation for his religion in a single verse, Micah 6:8. "God has shown you ... what is good and what the Lord requires of you. Do justly, love mercy, and walk humbly with your God." It is a single verse that is a life's work. All mastery runs to simplicity. All inadequacy self-inflates with compensatory complexity. Prevarication doth protest too much.

John Wayne said, "Life is hard. It's harder if you're stupid." An Old Breed Marine, Mr. Crow, said that if you're gonna be dumb you gotta be tough. Like the parable of the bridge builder and the sheep, I can do 1,000 smart things and nullify them by doing one incredibly stupid thing. While you are thinking of 1,000 smart things to do, remember to avoid the incredibly stupid.

Subtraction often beats addition. The difference between a crisis and an inconvenience is defined by the threat of devastation. In medical triage, a crisis is a threat to life, limb, or eyesight. The assessment determines the priorities of treatment. Mastery requires intimacy with essence and the elimination of the superfluous. Ancient wisdom advocates for the renunciation of *need*. VandenBroek said, "Every movement that humanity has made toward enlightenment and justice is in reality a movement toward simplicity of life."

In business, medicine, relationships, fitness, health, and life the attributes of soundness rely on knowing what matters and what does not. It is a revelation to understand how few things matter. Of those things that do, determining *how much* they matter is akin to a higher calling. They are the cornerstone of vitality.

> "If you seek tranquility, do less. Or (more accurately) do what's essential—what the logos of a social being requires, and in the requisite way. Which brings double satisfaction: do less, better. Because most of what we say and do is not essential. If you can eliminate it, you'll have more time and more tranquility. Ask yourself at every moment, 'Is this necessary?' But we need to eliminate unnecessary assumptions as well. To eliminate the unnecessary actions that follow . . . Don't be

disturbed. Uncomplicate yourself. Someone has done wrong . . . to himself. Something happens to you. Good. It was meant for you by nature, woven into the pattern from the beginning. Life is short. That's all there is to say. Get what you can from the present—thoughtfully, justly. Unrestrained moderation."[23]

Making Sense of Yourself. In Samuel Barondes' book *Making Sense of People*, he breaks down psychology for the proletariat. The lessons I learned began by taking my personal inventory and then observing others around me. The acronym O-C-E-A-N captures the five baseline bundles of 1,000s of personality traits, categorized into the following domains (pg. 16):

- <u>Openness (Closedness)</u>: curious/uninquisitive; sophisticated/unsophisticated; reflective/disinterested; Polar Nouns: innovator/traditionalist.
- <u>Conscientiousness (Disinhibition)</u>: reliable/unreliable; practical/impractical; hardworking/lazy; careful/negligent; organized/disorganized; Polar Nouns: workaholic/slacker.
- <u>Extraversion (Introversion)</u>: outgoing vs. shy; bold vs. reserved; talkative vs. quiet; Polar Nouns: the life of the party/loner.
- <u>Agreeableness (Antagonism)</u>: warm/cold; cooperative/uncooperative; trusting/suspicious;

---

[23] Aurelius, *Meditations*, 36-37.

generous/stingy; kind/unkind; Polar Nouns: altruist/misanthrope.

- <u>Neuroticism (Emotional Stability)</u>: tense/relaxed; unstable/stable; discontented/contented; irritable/imperturbable; histrionic/composed; Polar Nouns: whiner/cool cat.

We are not all one or all another. We can be middling, high, or low in traits. Our dispositions trend on a spectrum between poles. Mr. Barondes recommends the use of the "NEO-PI R" which was developed by Paul Costa and Robert McCrae at the National Institutes of Health. The personality test frames questions that evaluate facets within the Big 5 domains by making distinctions in degrees of six subdivided components within each Big 5. Understanding these five basic tendencies in relationships, and their facets, is vital to recognizing patterns in dynamics. I must know myself first.

A "personality disorder" is when one suffers from or is impaired or distressed by an extreme and inflexible form of one or more of the following patterns:[24]

1. **Antisocial**: disregard for and violation of the "rights" of others.
2. **Avoidant**: social inhibition, feelings of inadequacy, hypersensitivity to negative evaluation.
3. **Borderline**: instability in personal relationships, self-image, and emotions. Marked by impulsivity.

---

[24] S. Barondes, *Making Sense of People: Decoding The Mysteries Of Personality* (New York: FT Press, 2012), 30-31.

4. **Compulsive**: preoccupation with orderliness, perfectionism, and control.
5. **Dependent**: submissive and clinging related to an excessive need to be taken care of.
6. **Histrionic**: excessive emotionality and attention-seeking.
7. **Narcissistic**: grandiosity, need for admiration, lack of empathy.
8. **Paranoid**: distrust and suspiciousness such that others' motives are interpreted as malevolent.
9. **Schizoid**: detachment from social relationships and restricted range of emotional expression.
10. **Schizotypal**: acute discomfort in close relationships, cognitive or perceptual distortions, eccentricities of behavior.

Barondes offers much more in his book than a breakdown of psychological elements. He covers genetics, building a personal brain, tackles good character and identity, and closes with methods to put it all together toward personal health and happiness. Knowledge is good. Putting knowledge into action is better.

The Four Functions. "According to Jungian psychology, the human personality has four aspects, or *functions*, set in two opposing pairs. The first pair is thinking and feeling; the second pair is intuition and sensation. The first pair is rational, the second irrational."[25] Thinking is what you'd expect. It's what we think about things. Feeling

---

[25] R. Johnson, *Ecstasy: Understanding the Psychology of Joy* (New York: Harper and Row, 1987), 53.

incorporates emotions to evaluate things and situations. "Intuition implies a nonverbal, irrational perception of ideas, outcomes, and situations. Sensation has to do with a nonrational, sensate perception of the physical world of objects – their sizes, shapes, colors, smells, sounds."[26] From birth to early adulthood, our consciousness is formed as we activate these four functions.

An initial function is fired up early, a second sometime during adolescence, and, as we are able, a third. The function that comes most naturally is called a *superior function*.[27] The least used or unused function is the *inferior function*. For the function that comes most naturally, we "specialize" in it. We have the most control over superior functions and the least control over inferior functions. Our superior function is well-developed, and our inferior remains undeveloped. Johnson points out that this is "a greatly simplified explanation ... no one exemplifies these functions as clearly in real life as it is possible to do in theory."

Theoretically, then, a human who has brought into consciousness all four functions is enlightened. It's a rare occurrence. The dawn of the fourth function threatens the Ego and often brings with it confusion, disorder, structural breakdown, and erratic behavior. "The fourth function is the representation of the unlived life we still contain."[28] It is not surprising that the fourth function's demand for

---

[26] Ibid., 53-54
[27] Ibid.
[28] Ibid., 55.

inclusion occurs around the age of 45, commensurate with what many experience as a "midlife crisis."

Johnson explains that when our superior function has been drained of much of its energy over a lifetime of use in the lead position, the inferior function retains the full power of its primal energy. The clash of these two functions can be disastrous, as the superior function – through the Ego – no longer has the power to enforce behavioral or interpretive frameworks that have served us our entire lives. The inferior function "with all its unlived energy" rises from the deep and breaks the surface spectacularly.

"Any repressed material in our personalities automatically begins to revolve around our inferior functions." Summarized from *Ecstasy*:[29]

- Thinking. The dominant function in our fact-oriented society; make informed opinions about situations; when tossing and turning at 3 a.m. you are subjected to your feeling function. The whole orgiastic, out-of-control, vague-yearning-for-tropical-paradise quality comes rushing up by way of your inferior function.

- Feeling. Has rational perceptions on the emotional level and will judge things as comfortable or uncomfortable, wonderful or awful, according to how they feel in the moment. You may construct utopias and gardens of Eden three times a week – but they come down as easily as they go up!

---

[29] Ibid.., 56-57.

- <u>Sensing</u>. You are at ease with the physical world. You know the size, shape, color, texture, and location of the objects and beings around you without having to think about them consciously. Intuition is your inferior function... you may have a difficult time handling the unknown, populating the future with the out-of-control figures of your intuition.
- <u>Intuition</u>. Perceive the total situation irrationally – its background, present, and likely outcome. ... You form general impressions, and abstract ideas, rather than concrete detail, and sensing is your inferior function.

"You may tax your superior function to the limit, and it will always see you through. But you must protect your inferior function at all costs because it goes wild under pressure."

Regardless of whether you're 45 and experiencing the turmoil of a midlife crisis, the opportunity to recruit energy, creativity, new life, and ecstasy abides. Carl Jung posited that our connections with God reside in the inferior function, for that is where we lack control. We don't find God in the manicured, managed constructs of our internal estates, but in the wild badlands beyond our fences. In the same way that Taoism encourages keeping one foot in the known and one in the unknown –The Way— we must not hide or flee from our inferior functions. We can create space for them to manifest and draw from their vast stores of unexpended energy in ways that do not wreak havoc in our lives.

My superior functions are thinking and intuiting. My inferior function is sensing. At least, I *think* that's what it is! In one of my professional roles, I unwittingly tapped into the world of sensation and was delighted to find a new kind of fulfillment in the work. As an operating officer responsible for the daily operations of four restaurants, my superior thinking function enabled the effective ordering, planning, training, and execution of numerous activities with myriad levels of complexity.

In addition, there were requirements to oversee the physical facilities and the maintenance of equipment. As a small enterprise, we couldn't afford a full-time person to perform those tasks, so I took them on. The world of physical things, the pieces and parts of machinery and how they work together, electricity and plumbing, water and air pressure balances, and filtration and lubrication were foreign affairs for me. Although I grew up in a family of construction professionals and had overseen military programs requiring maintenance activities, I had rarely been the one *doing the work.*

I knew ideas and principles around these functions, but learning to solve problems and resolve them with my hands using physical objects opened a new world to me. I had always believed that my brother, a professional and expert commercial and residential builder, had gotten the "gene" for that and I had not. I learned that, though it may not come easily or naturally to me, my inferior function can be exercised and energized in ways that are fulfilling. On many occasions (but not all), confronting a confounding equipment malfunction, I was able to disassemble an object, understand how the parts worked together, determine the problem, and fix it.

Without any training, the result of many of my fixes became affectionately known as the "hillbilly" solution. Any professional coming in behind me might scratch her head, wondering how I devised such a configuration. In my mind, if it worked it was good. I stood in quiet admiration of many completed projects, quietly laughing at the creative plumbing assembly or the field-expedient workaround I employed to keep things going. I realized along the way that I *can* do things like this, I simply haven't. Our inferior functions are not intrinsically limiting factors, they simply have not been developed. My experience fixing physical things taught me that through the fumbling and frustration of using a function with which I am unfamiliar, I can grow to love its expression.

The work was satisfying in a way that thinking work cannot be. I will never have a fully actuated sensing function the way my brother does, but I can intentionally cultivate it toward inclusion in who I am, both honoring and expressing it. The path to wholeness requires it.

On Personality, Talents, Hardwiring, and Quirks. Personality tests provide insight into how we are wired and what makes us tick. Large organizations, the military, and special occupations of many kinds include personality tests as tools to assist with talent management, team organization, coaching, and selection for specific roles. For individuals, personality "typing" enables understanding of how we best learn and process information, our natural strengths and weaknesses, and how we make decisions. Understanding your personality type illuminates patterns. The recognition of patterns is essential to analyzing the "systems" operating in your life. As a bonus, personality tests are fun to do with your friends, if you're into that sort of thing.

In Jungian psychology, archetypes represent universal patterns and images that are part of the collective unconscious. From Jung's work, the archetypes he established form the basis for many personality tests. For Jung, archetypes recognized behavioral patterns observable across time and space, in our collective human history, familiar in myth, story, and religion spanning eras. Archetypal figures and images appear often in dreams, art, and talismans. The 12 Jungian archetypes are:

- The Innocent
- Everyman
- Hero
- Outlaw
- Explorer
- Creator
- Ruler
- Magician
- Lover
- Caregiver
- Jester
- Sage

From these archetypes, modern personality studies have evolved, as have the tests that assess them. The Enneagram arranges nine personality types into three "Centers"; the clinical Sixteen Personality Factor Questionnaire (16PF) uncovers 16 central elements and scores them on a spectrum (more like this, less like that) and is used by advanced psychologists; and, the Myers-Briggs framework consists of eight preferences organized into four pairs of opposites.[30]

Understanding your personality type is not a hall pass to let you off the hook. "That's just how I am" is an inadequate justification for failure to adapt, petulance, or laziness. In many cases, such tests uncover ingrained preferences or conditioning as often as they do hard wiring. I tend to find my weaknesses more fascinating than my strengths because they highlight blind spots. Detractors of psychological personality profiling point toward a societal obsession with weaknesses, conditions, labels, and other justifications that provide glib "reasons" why I can't do better. In rigorous scientific circles, personality tests are considered pseudoscience. Nevertheless, their popularity ebbs and flows.

Marcus Buckingham and Donal O. Clifton, Ph.D., in *Now, Discover Your Strengths*, based on over two million Gallup Organization interviews, the authors seek to shift the reader's focus from shoring up weaknesses to developing strengths. They debunk two flawed assumptions, 1) anybody can learn to be competent in

---

[30] www.myersbriggs.org

almost anything, and 2) that the potential for personal growth is greatest in areas of weakness. Conversely, they offer that we are each wired with enduring and unique strengths, or "talents", and that our areas of greatest growth potential are found in the areas of these talents. In short, instead of building my life, my aspirations, and my medical profile around my weaknesses, I will fare better if I pour resources into my strengths, giving my weaknesses only the attention required to prevent them from becoming liabilities.

Additionally, it is not true that I can be anything I want. Each of us has talents that can take us as far as our limitations will allow, but these talents will not ensure success equally in any chosen endeavor. I will always be better at some things than others. Choosing careers based on strengths gives me a better shot at becoming good at it. Most of our heroes are great, even the best ever, at one thing or a particular constellation of things   that produce one thing.

Strengths and weaknesses are two sides of the same coin. An example of my talents, per the Strengths Finder profile, is Activator. The Activator exhibits a compelling bias toward action. Activators believe that we learn best in motion, through action and experience. An Activator has a high tolerance for risk and will act without having fully considered every possible risk or roadblock. This talent can come across as impatience. Action is good, except when premature.

Understanding my Activator tendencies has enabled me to become a better analyst, a beneficial skill during planning and decision-making. Though I will never suffer from paralysis through analysis, understanding that I am compelled to decide and act as quickly as possible has given me the wisdom to slow down when things are important. The qualities of an Activator are strengths in many contexts, but a hasty decision without vital information can lead to disaster. From this, I have devised mental frameworks to approach planning and decision-making to ensure that I do my homework before I release the hounds. I will share more on this framework shortly.

A therapist I knew rarely answered questions directly. Instead, she'd say, "You may want to be curious about that." Personality tests and understanding your strengths don't answer all your questions about how to organize and run a well-ordered life or how to succeed in business, but they give you a lot to be curious about. Knowing *what* you want is crucial. Knowing *why* you want it is revelatory.

Complex Problem-Solving. In both my professional and personal life, devising a reliable system to plan and solve problems has proven invaluable. I am the fortunate recipient of education and experience in military decision-making, special operations strategic planning, and the mentorship of numerous officers, non-commissioned officers, and executives who have taught me to simplify complexity, prioritize and decide, and sketch a solid plan. I once worked for a CEO who required that I reduce a problem set to a single sentence.

His format for an executive summary was one sentence each for 1) The problem, 2) Why it matters, and 3) The proposed solution, for a total of three sentences. He taught me that if I cannot reduce a problem to a single sentence, I either don't know what the problem is or it is more than one problem. What follows is a distillation of many planning and decision-making systems into my own. In planning, systems and problems are reduceable to elements. I use the word element to denote irreducible parts. When understanding actions or the function of a running system to make improvements or forecast results, you must consider *causation* and *correlation*.

A simple example in military planning is an assault on an objective. The opposition (enemy) is doing something on the objective that I don't want them to do, e.g., an illegal armed group is stealing food from a village near their base camp. I plan to stop it. Causative factors in planning mean that if I do "X" I expect a "Y" result. Correlative factors are those results determined by a measure of effectiveness, or 2nd and 3rd order effects, e.g., *more* or *less* of a thing. In this example, I lead a company of gunfighters to the enemy camp and clear it. The stealing stops because the opposing combatants are gone (causative). Additionally, the local population feels safer and the relationship of my unit with the populace improves. From that relationship comes increasingly reliable intelligence (correlative).

When taking stock of my life and creating an action plan, I advocate a *top-down* approach. Conversely, to learn the art of "Stress-free Productivity" (managing task lists, information, and projects), I swear by David Allen's *bottom-up* approach explained in his book *Getting Things Done*. For my life map, I've found no better terminology to denote levels than the military *strategic, operational,* and *tactical*. My life at the strategic level captures the overall trajectory (where I am heading) and the big buckets that make my life what it is. Examples are my profession, spouse/family, home, health, finances, physical capacity, and spiritual connection. Since my life is a system of systems, each of these categories is a system of its own.

Operations occur within each of these categories and tactics are the concrete, specific actions taken to achieve the operational objective. Each of these systems is perfectly designed to yield the results that I am getting. As I examine them, I find many areas where improvements could be made. My approach is not to "be better about things", but to identify specific systems (or lack thereof) that yield results I want to change. Like the difference between shouting "Call 9-1-1" to a crowd around an emergency and pointing directly at a single person and saying, "*You* call 9-1-1", generalizations are ineffective; precision is essential. Without a pointed "you", no one calls 9-1-1. Health provides an easy example. If I'm 50 pounds overweight, I suffer consequences in my daily life. If I commit to a crash diet to lose weight, whether I lose it is irrelevant if I fail to address systemic issues.

I gained weight because a combination of systems at work in my life are designed to yield weight gain. One such system is how, when, and what I feed myself. Habits, emotions, laziness, external influences, and ignorance all play roles. Another system is my level of physical activity.

If I have a desk job and a sedentary lifestyle, the lack of a fitness system plays a role. If I go on a caloric restriction diet and lose weight, that is a causative action. A correlation is when my blood pressure goes down, a health benefit. Another correlation is that my favorite jeans fit again! This is all good, but if I haven't addressed the systemic issues my jeans will again be too small within six months. Let's break it down using a simplified approach that I call the FICSS-It plan:

Framing, Imaging, Curating/Coordinating, Sequencing, and Synchronization.

PROBLEM-SOLVING (FICSS IT PLAN)
FRAMING: (Define the Problem) What's the gap between current and desired
IMAGING: (Anticipate) Quantify Success & Visualize Road blocks
CURATING/COORDINATING: (Action the Gap) Cross functional recruitment; gather resources, knowledge, or supporting elements
SEQUENCING: Set priorities; set timelines; map critical path
SYNCHRONIZATION: (Ownership/Tracking)Standardize operational tempo, plan communications (frequency, format, and method), and establish mutual accountability

- **FRAMING (Define the Problem)**
  - The problem is that I've gained weight.

- The gap is 50 pounds = the delta between my current weight and my desired weight.

- **IMAGING (Quantify Success & Visualize Roadblocks)**
  - Quantify Succes: I will have succeeded when I weigh "X", which is 50 pounds lighter than I currently weigh.
  - Visualize Roadblocks:
    - I eat lunch out most days with my co-workers. It's a productive time. If I bring my lunch, it would be weird to bring a brown sack to a restaurant, but I don't want to miss the discussions.
    - I'm not sure what I ought to eat.
    - My wife cooks most of our dinners. I know she doesn't want to go on a diet because she's fit as a fiddle!
    - I don't have time to eat breakfast in the morning.
    - I don't have time to meal prep.
    - Working out sucks, I don't know what I'm doing, and a gym membership is too expensive. A trainer is way too expensive.
    - I drive a lot for work and like to have my snacks.
    - The men's cookout on game day won't be as fun without beer and nachos.
    - The universe will conspire against me in 1,000s of unforeseeable ways.

- **CURATING/COORDINATING (Action the Gap – gather resources, knowledge, support)**
  - Call Steve. He lost a lot of weight last year and kept it off. Ask him how he did it and enlist his support.
  - Research sustainable nutritional programs (NOT crash diets), something I can reasonably *live with*.
  - Inventory my pantry and get rid of stuff that I won't be able to resist.
  - When I say I don't "have" time, I mean that I don't make time. Once I know what I'm going to eat every day, I'll figure out a time during the weekend to put it all together for the following week.
  - Talk to my wife about my plan. She'll want me to shed some pounds and we can figure out together how to arrange meals so that I can eat them in part or whole.
  - Walking is free. I'll get up 45 minutes earlier every morning and take a 30-minute walk before everyone wakes up. That way I'll get it done every day.
  - Game Day cookout: once I have my plan together, I'll let the lads know. If they're true friends, they'll ultimately support me even though they'll give me a hard time. If they're just drinking buddies, they don't get a vote about how I live my life. They're in or they're out.
  - If the universe throws me a surprise (donuts at work!), I'll take one back to my desk and throw it away.

- **SEQUENCING (Prioritize, Establish Timelines, Map Critical Path)**
  - Milestones/Indicators: average 3 pounds lost weight per week. I won't worry about a week where I only lose two pounds and I won't think I've crossed the finish line when I lose four pounds.
  - I'll start my nutrition correction program on the first day of next month, which gives me three weeks to figure it out. I don't have to wait to start walking. I'll start tomorrow.
    - Week One: call Steve and get smart on nutrition. Learn ways to order healthy meals in restaurants so that I can eat with my co-workers at least twice a week.
    - Week Two: Talk to my wife, organize my pantry, and talk to the lads.
    - Week Three: Schedule meal prep time and go shopping. Stock my house with things I can eat and don't forget healthy snacks for the car!

- **Synchronization (Ownership, Accountability, and Tracking)**
  - Daily Journal: at the end of each day, I'll capture notes on nutrition (what I ate and how much), any slip-ups, overall mood, and any signs of the changes, e.g., skin, hair, energy levels, mental clarity, sleep quality, how I felt on my walk.
  - Weekly: I'll weigh myself and take a front and side picture of myself for the archives.

- Weekly: after I've weighed, if I haven't lost three pounds, I'll review my journal to see how closely I stuck to my plan. If I can determine causative variables, adjust. If not, give it another week. If I stick to my plan for two weeks with no weight loss, talk to Steve and evaluate the program (caloric intake, hydration, sugar, starch) and adjust.

The FICSS-it framework produces scalable, actionable, feasible, and sustainable plans. It establishes an operational line of effort (LOE) (lose weight) and converts that idea into concrete tasks reduced to single actions and prioritized (sequenced) for efficiency and progression. An operational line of effort for our purposes in this book is a mapped, prioritized, and sequenced series of actions (sequential or concurrent) conducted toward a measurable or precisely articulated end state. A line of effort is also nested within and supports strategic imperatives.

You must quantify tasks as well as possible, meaning that they must be specific enough that you know when they have been accomplished. The mapping of operational lines of effort across strategic imperatives is a classic military method to organize complexity. The breakdown of specific tactical tasks into unique "next" and "waiting" actions is a David Allen technique. In this example, the LOE directly supports the strategic imperative of overall wellness through weight loss (causative). It also indirectly supports medical health and longevity (correlative). The FICSS-it plan can be applied to multiple LOEs to produce an overarching strategic plan for continued improvement.

Our dilemma is often not the result of a lack of knowledge, but a lack of vision, organization, discipline, and heart. It all feels like too much to handle. It can feel overwhelming. Life is complex. I'm afraid. How do I simplify it so that I know what to do next? This simple problem-solving, prioritization, and execution framework is an effective tool. If used thoughtfully and consistently, it accomplishes the alchemic conversion of ideas into action and action into tangible results. A "vision board" or an ideas journal is great but incomplete. The magic is turning the ethereal into material. Strategy without tactics is the slowest march to victory (Sun Tzu); operations occur at the speed of trust (General Mattis); and tactics without strategy are the noise prior to defeat (Sun Tzu).

At best, this chapter has served as a primer. An introduction to ideas and reference to expert authors is insufficient to materialize a vision. Entire books and fields of study revolve around any number of the topics discussed here. Before fully committing to an endeavor, it is wise to understand as much about it as possible or at least enough to prevent needless floundering. Take stock of yourself and then your situation. Dive into what matters most. Learn more. Listen to people who know what they're talking about and keep studying. Develop a critical ear, especially toward your internal voice(s).

Weigh and scrutinize. Choose what you believe. Discard trivia. Do the work. A good friend of mine, "Tugboat" Evans, asks the questions, "What? So what? What now?" Choose what's in your best interest, both personally and as a contributing citizen, map a plan, and commit. Know *what* you are after and *why*. Decide what needs to start and what needs to stop. Get a handle on a thing or two and get after it. How long will you wait until you demand from yourself the best version of yourself?

4

Commitment (Disciplined Doing)

"As life is action and passion, it is required of a man that he should share the passion and action of his time at peril of being judged not to have lived."

– Oliver Wendell Holmes

Commitment Defined. Involvement or participation differs from commitment. In the case of making a ham and cheese omelet, the chicken was involved; the pig was committed (J.D. Crow).

"Chuck" was a U.S. Marine infantry commander in Vietnam. I met Chuck in my local gym when I was getting in shape to attend USMC Officer Candidate School (OCS). The attrition rate at the time in Marine OCS was over 50%. My class, which started in January, purportedly broke records for the coldest winter in Virginia. We were losing candidates so quickly that the school commander intervened to determine what was happening. By the end, almost 60% of our class had dropped on request or been sent home by the cadre. I'd heard stories about how tough it was before I arrived, so

I knew I needed to prepare physically in a way I never had. The farthest distance I had ever run was after a lucky catch I made during a football game followed by an 80-

yard dash to the endzone. At OCS, you run everywhere and, some days, you run until the *instructors* get tired. The physical fitness test itself included a three-mile run. I was nervous. I had a lot of work to do. Chuck saw me doing 100s of push-ups, pull-ups, and sit-ups. He broke the ice by asking, "What are you training for?" When I told him, he said, "I recognized the workout."

Chuck (R.I.P) and I got to know each other. He discovered I was studying English and creative writing and asked if I'd read a draft book he'd written. The book was about his experience in Vietnam. During Chuck's first tour in Vietnam, he commanded a company of infantry Marines. The life expectancy of infantry Marines in Vietnam was short, counted as days or weeks sometimes, but Chuck thrived in that environment. One day, a visitor spoke with his company about a new, nameless unit, given only an alpha-numeric designator, and invited volunteers to join. It was dangerous, thankless, covert work that required additional training and immediate follow-on tours in Vietnam.

Chuck signed up for what later became U.S. Marine Force Reconnaissance. His unpublished book detailed the missions that he and his small teams conducted. They were harrowing, heartbreaking, and bloody. Chuck recounted the time he heard the President of the United States insist to the American public that there were no U.S. troops in Cambodia. Chuck heard this on the radio *while on a mission in Cambodia.* He burned French drug plantations, assassinated enemy officers, and carried out unspeakable missions in the grey zones of ethics and laws of war.

Following Vietnam, Chuck became a Judge Advocate General (JAG) in the Marines and translated that into a civilian career as a lawyer and real estate developer in California and Hawaii. A few years after he left active duty, an old friend of his asked if he was interested in doing "side work." Chuck and his friend met in the parking lot of a fast-food restaurant. In the trunk of the man's car, he showed Chuck an array of weapons systems, gadgetry, and technology.

Chuck joined the Agency as a special missions operator, unknown to anyone, including his wife. His travel for business provided a solid alibi. Chuck's wife discovered his side hustle when she returned home early and found him unpacking from a "work trip", like a scene out of a movie. He said, "She walked into our bedroom, looked around, and silently walked out." On the bed, laid out were hard cases of weapons and equipment and a duffel bag full of cash. In the closet, the door to a secret compartment under the floor was open. Chuck's wife gave him an ultimatum. He promised he wouldn't do any more missions. He did anyway, and they eventually divorced.

When I knew Chuck, he was in his late sixties and early seventies. He was retired, lived in a small condo alone, and rode his bike everywhere. Anytime we met for lunch, it was at an Asian restaurant. He always ate stir-fried vegetables and white rice, no salt and no sauce. He drank tea and water and nothing else. He had an irrepressible sense of humor and a gleam in his eye. After everything he had done, seen, and earned, Chuck found his peace in the simplest version of life, a quiet, active, and profound man slipping silently unseen through mobs of everyday people, the consummate warrior-monk-poet.

Lunch with Chuck was akin to visiting an oracle. As easygoing and conversational as he was, everything he said was worth careful consideration. After my first tour in the Marines, I joined an infantry battalion as a reservist. Chuck was dying. He invited me to his house. It was the last time I saw Chuck alive. He called me because he wanted to impart some wisdom to me before he journeyed to the other side. I sat with him briefly in his living room and then sat by his bed when he was too tired to sit up. Without looking at me, lying on his back watching the ceiling fan, he said, "Fight the Company." I repeated it as a question. "Yes. Fight the Company," he said. Chuck told me that as a commander, I have one job.

That job is to wield a company of the greatest fighting force the world has ever known to win battles. He told me that a commander is bombarded with competing urgencies. Boiled down to the essence, an effective commander maintains situational awareness, allocates resources, and makes decisions quickly so that his Marines are free to do what they're trained to do: shoot, move, and communicate. That's it. In true Chuck style, he said, "If you're doing anything else, you're not doing your job. You're f**king it up and you'll get Marines killed." Don't complicate it. Stay in the fight. Do your job. Fight the company.

Hermann Melville wrote that "in times of peril, like the needle to the lodestone, obedience, irrespective of rank, generally flies to him best fitted for command." In the parlance of our times (ref. Big Lebowski), when the shit hits the fan, everybody looks to the person they trust to get them out of their jam. Leadership like that is not *positional* (rank-based), it's *relational* (trust-based). It's not given freely. You earn it.

The Marine leadership motto is *ductus exemplo*, leadership by example. Commitment to the calling you accept, including that of becoming an "imminently qualified human being" (Jocko), requires that you become the type of person who people can count on during a crisis. You must also build enough self-trust that you can rely on yourself in times of trouble to decipher a workable solution amid uncertainty. Self-leadership is inextricably linked to self-trust. In ordinary lives, those far less remarkable than Chuck's, there will be sickness, loss, grave mistakes, funerals, hard times, accidents, and tragedy.

There will be wobbly wheels and fiery crashes, explosions, implosions, and meltdowns. Becoming the type of person who is reliable during rough patches is a lofty aspiration and not easily earned. The individual human being is a "company" all its own, with varying capabilities, complementary systems, limitations, and prime functions. You have one job, which is to maximize the effectiveness of *You* as a constellation of capabilities, raw power, and adaptable capacities. Your rational mind is the commander. It has one job. You are the captain of your soul.

Notes on (Self-) Leadership. Positional leadership is an appointment. Relational leadership is earned. If I'm the smartest person in the room, I need different people in the room or I'm in the wrong room. Mark Twain said, "Comparison is the death (or thief) of joy." Don't think of yourself as an "Alpha", as in "alpha male." I mention this because my military experience was replete with the compensatory signaling of alpha status amongst those least likely to outperform their peers. Being needlessly antagonistic and combative while sporting a severe haircut does not an alpha make. Professions of alpha status and the statistical likelihood of mediocre performance were directly proportional, based on personal observation. Like a nickname, the designation of alpha status is earned and is decided by your team, not yourself.

Moreover, such labeling categorically misses the point. Alphas compete against others for dominance. You must compete against yourself, not against others. Granted, in certain scenarios, we are measured against others by an external entity, or evaluated, even ranked, among a group of peers, but that is outside our control. Notwithstanding, I must resist any urge to do the same. Compare your *today* self to your *yesterday* self *only*, not to others and not to your *tomorrow* self. Do your best, put yourself last, and let your work speak for itself. Lead yourself. As a soldier climbs through tiers of military units, from conventional to special to elite, he discovers that self-leadership and self-motivation are tested to the extreme. Benchmarks of performance and standards of time are unpublished. Selectees accomplish tasks with minimal information and no feedback on how they're doing. In an environment stripped of comparative markers, both quantified (time cut-offs) and relative to other humans (you're in the woods alone), the admonition to "do your best" means exactly that. It is the only metric by which you can measure your performance. In the end, you find out if your best effort satisfied their requirements. Don't compare yourself to others. Cultivate internal standards that exceed external expectations. Then, while the "alphas" around you butt heads and bluster, you can save energy and focus on your work.

If you find yourself leading others, look back to ensure someone is following you. If not, you're just out on a stroll. If people are following you, dedicate yourself to serving them. Provide resources and remove obstacles. Earn trust. As a USMC 2nd lieutenant at The Basic School, the cadre rotates students through leadership positions at different levels, from Fire Team Leader (team of four) to Company Commander (250 Marines).

The rotation lasts two weeks and the cadre, as well as your fellow students, grade you on your performance and potential. The unforgivable sin is selfishness. I was the student platoon sergeant (50 Marines) during a 20-mile ruck march. Every hour or so, we'd pause so that guys could reconfigure gear, change socks, patch blisters, and get a snack. I was at the front during a halt when the water cans came off the truck. In the interest of efficiency, I figured I'd fill my canteens quickly and then walk the line to check on the platoon. The Sheriff, the nickname that my buddy B.C. gave our staff platoon commander, our captain, asked what

I was doing. "Filling up, sir, then going to check on the lads." He sarcastically said, "Good plan. That's what Marines need, a well-fed, well-hydrated, and well-rested leader." Then he said, without sarcasm, "Check on them first. After that, if there's any water left, maybe you'll have time to get some. Maybe not." Roger that.

Simon Sinek based *Leaders Eat Last* on the leadership advice of proven combat leaders. The principle seems self-evident, but, even in the military, it is rarely fully embodied by leaders and manifests in degrees, with the best leaders in my experience expressing it most fully. Leadership is service to others. Sinek noted that the cost of leadership is self-interest. When an airplane is falling out of the sky, you put your oxygen mask on first, then help others. Self-leadership is also service, mature leadership of my system of systems toward that which is most healthy for me, most effective, and most natural. It is *stewardship*. Self-leadership requires that my prefrontal cortex – my rational mind – acts as the adult and leads the other parts of me in directions that are *in my best interest*.

A psychologist that I saw for over a year, Dr. Bicknell, a referral from the Department of Veteran's Affairs, told me that often. Doing what is in my best interest is not the same thing as doing what I want. Often, they are vastly different. I must attend to those things that usher the totality of my being toward a healthier and more functional version. My adult mind must also resist and fend off alternatives, regardless of how enticing they are. Fifteen miles into a ruck march with a heavy pack, I'm as tired and thirsty as everyone else. The difference between "everyone else" and the "platoon sergeant" is that the leader is responsible for the platoon first, before himself. The unit is more important than the individual.

In the same way, who I am to myself, my community, and the planet is more important than the demands that my six-year-old self (brain stem, cerebellum, and basal ganglia) makes or the fits he pitches. Your rational mind is the platoon sergeant of the rest of your systems and is responsible for ensuring that they are led with care. The platoon sergeant decides that the platoon is going on a 20-mile ruck and everyone goes. He is also responsible for providing what is needed to ensure safety and the successful completion of the exercise. Decide where you are going and the rest of you will follow, though parts of yourself may complain. Along the way, take care of yourself. Lead yourself. You are your brother's keeper.

I Want to Know What Love Is (or Love is the Only Weapon). I believe that authentic love is goodwill oriented toward the existential locus of another as they *are* and as they *are not yet,* willing for them only what is good from now through eternity. Simply, I want the best for you, whatever that happens to be, even when I don't know what the best is. In this way, I can love someone whom I do not like. In critical circumstances, love will *demand* the best and will not tolerate self-sabotage, half-truths, or delusional thoughts, feelings, and behavior. I love you as you are, but I don't accept you "just as you are." You're better than that. I respect you too much. I love you for all that you are *and* for all that you could be. I recognize in you vast, unexplored geographies of potential and beauty. A topographical map of the heart reveals the highest peaks and the deepest valleys. A journey through it is to gasp at expansive views from mountaintops and to shiver in the shadow of death. I want for you all that you have and all that you could ever have. More importantly, I cherish who you are and who you are becoming.

Practically, I believe that love-in-action is not transactional. It is not a condition, it is not the constellation of feelings associated with it, nor is it something into which I unwittingly fall.

Romantic love and modern conceptions of its meaning were first developed sometime around the twelfth century in Europe. From it, myths surrounding damsels in distress and heroic knights became the standard against which mundane human love is measured. But they are not the same thing. Romantic devotion came to mean sworn allegiance to the idealized maiden, undying fealty, and heart-stricken pursuit, i.e., "courting." In its purest form, the maiden was both *untouched* and *untouchable*.

Even human sexuality wilted in the radiance of the maiden, for the too-human function of copulation became viewed as base and sordid. Hence, pure romantic love was stripped of primal sexual drive and elevated to that of devotion for devotion's sake. Romance is the perpetual pursuit of an ideal that is never attainable. Before these mythical constructs, Joseph Campbell explains in *The Power of Myth* that "Love was simply Eros, the god who excites you to sexual desire." The cultivation of romantic love during this time elevated the concept to divine status and discarded elements of natural temporal "profanity."

It was no longer humanly relational, but a form of divine worship. They took sex out of love and made it religion. St. Francis of Assisi, the son of a wealthy merchant who devoted himself to poverty, was a paragon of romantic love. Francis did not simply relinquish his inheritance and become a monk, he created "Lady Poverty", to whom he swore his consecrated fidelity and penned lavish love poems. The idea was powerful enough that Francis soon had hundreds of followers and later thousands, for romantic devotion carried the weight of the highest ideal of the time.

The delusion of romantic love persists. Robert Johnson's treatment of the topic from psychological and mythical perspectives is illuminating. He describes the onset of what we think of as love and falling into it as a high-voltage experience. We project our ideal onto our chosen object, hook ourselves to the main breaker, and positively surge with enough energy to light a city block. We elevate him or her, unknown to them (though they often do the same thing to us), onto a pedestal of mythic status. Inevitably, she will fall from that pedestal.

Ordinary life will ensure that fantasy becomes human. The bursting of the romantic bubble can take time to occur, but it undoubtedly will. It's shocking to realize that I didn't marry a woman, I married an ideal, but the ideal has evaporated and I live with another human being. Now what? Sadly, this often marks the end of a relationship or results in a relationship devoid of energy, magic, or "spark." We lament. Conversely, it is an invitation to connect as humans and to cultivate a sustainable and natural sharing of each other and our ordinary lives. We are returned to earth and invited to lend a hand to a fellow earthling and walk the dirt together.

As I commit to growth, it is essential to avoid "falling in love" with a grand image of my idealized self. I am human and my image of myself must be a human one. Most of what occurs in life cannot be controlled. Feeble attempts to exert control beyond myself remind me that I am no deified ideal, I'm just some dude trying to not screw it up so badly that I can't recover. The common variable in all my failed relationships is me, but I dismiss this fact because "you" did not measure up. But it's always me. That said, sometimes it's you too. Nobody measures up to an idealized, composite version of the qualities I worship. I am vulnerable to the same delusions concerning self-love. Acceptance of our humanness is the first step toward relating authentically. Within a human framework, I can establish realistic notions. I can work toward achievable ends.

In the economy of the universe, "God's economy", there is always enough. In the "everything" of the universe, comparison is an irrelevant notion. Transactions are comparative. Human love in its best form is not transactional, as when I give you something because you give me something. Active human love requires no scoreboard because it is not a 50/50 arrangement. If anything, it's 100/0, each side offering all that they have without the expectation of return. The most observable embodiment of love closest to this is that of a parent for a child. Children are unable to reciprocate for years and yet parents continue to pour themselves into their children.

The object of this type of love, a child, is often thought to be the primary beneficiary. Closer observation reveals that our deepest motivations to love our children are more about us than them. The principles of "I get what I give", or "I reap what I sow", are axiomatic in healthy parent-child relationships. I *experience* them and can attest to their truth. Translated into a couple's version of non-transactional love, instead of searching for the perfect partner, I seek instead to become the best partner I can be. My mindset shifts from holding you responsible for my unmet needs to providing what you need. Instead of coming to you with an empty cup, and asking you to fill it, I come to you with a full cup, asking if you're thirsty (I think Will Smith said that or something like it). When I love like this, you benefit, but it is I who receives the greatest reward.

In the trenches of a relationship, including my relationship with myself, there is nothing too small or too big to argue about. At the beginning of our marriage, I told my wife to immediately tell me when a quirk of mine, if it's within my control to change it, bothers her. "Darling, if you don't like the way I slurp soup out of a spoon, tell me now. If you don't, one day you'll snatch the spoon out of my hand and stab me in the ocular cavity with it."

Clarify your true stance on irritants, because you must immediately address them or let them go forever. Committing to growth requires the willingness to address what must be addressed, to relinquish that which is inconsequential, or beyond control, and to hold myself and others to *human* standards. Decide which hill you will die on. Suspended between the kinetic order of Heaven and the potential energy of Hell, we earthen vessels are a collision of what we were, what we are, and what we are to become. We are divine and profane, exquisite and messy, sparks from the divine flame, wearing suits of carbon-based dust.

On Trust. Do you trust yourself? I once attended a motivational workshop that had a cult-like, scream therapy, astrophysical flavor to it. A friend bought me a ticket and suggested I experience it. The leader instructed the class that "trust is a yes or no question." In context, he was asking us to trust him and his process. I ignored the illogical conflations that prefaced that statement, his dubious semantics, and went along for the ride. It was memorable. My experience has taught me that trust is *not* a yes or no question.

Abraham Maslow is famous for his hierarchy of human needs. Maslow also introduced a pyramid of trust. Related to human need, trust climbed a pyramid commensurate with having escalating tiers of needs met. The hierarchy of needs begins with foundational physiological needs (air, food, water, and shelter) and climbs the tiers of Safety and Security, Love and Belonging, and Self-esteem, and culminates with Self-Actualization (morality, creativity, acceptance, purpose, and inner potential). Similarly, the Pyramid of Trust begins with a baseline relevance that essential needs can be met, then moves upward through Interest and preference over other options, into trust with personal information, then with sensitive (e.g., financial or medical) information, and culminates with a willingness to invest in an ongoing relationship – to *commit*.

Stage theory, the clean linear progression from one level to another, fails to capture the reality that trust is developed simultaneously among the stages in degrees. I earn trust in all the stages at once in different proportions. If you flip the pyramid on its side and smash it flat, the vertical bar graph created is a more accurate visual depiction. (Thank you, Dr. Bicknell)

Commitment requires the highest level of trust. I must earn trust in myself in the same way that I earn it with others, through demonstrative integrity. As stated previously, I define integrity as the alignment between words (spoken and unspoken) and corresponding actions. I say what I mean, I mean what I say, and I do what I say in a meaningful way. Unintentionally, that rhymed. Integrity means wholeness. Stockdale wrote, "Integrity is a powerful word that derives from a specific concept. It describes a person who is *integrated*, blended into a *whole*, as opposed to a person of many parts, many faces, many disconnects. The word relates to the ancients' distinction between *living* and *living well*. ... He knows himself, reflects a definite and thoughtful set of preferences and aspirations, and is thus *reliable* [italics added]. Knowing he is whole, he is not preoccupied with riding the crest of continual anxiety but is free to ride the crest of *delight with life!*"[31]

Since trust is not an all-at-once episode, I earn it by keeping my word to myself. If I tell myself that I will endure seven days without sugar, I don't eat sugar for seven days, no matter what. One variable in my encouragement to start small is in the interest of trust. If I commit to something and deliver on it, I begin to establish trust. When I shoot for the moon right out of the gate, failure to deliver on my stated goals undermines trust.

The more I do what I say I will do, the more I trust myself. Ultimately, I will no more break a promise to myself than I would a promise to my best friend or brother. Scripture encourages us to be faithful (trustworthy) in small things if ever we are to be trusted with big things. Start small. Stack some wins. Build your follow-through muscle until it's strong enough to carry heavier weight. Be mindful to not say things that you know you won't do. Once you say them, you owe it to yourself to deliver. The burgeoning faith in yourself requires it. Keeping a promise is one step forward. Breaking a promise is ten steps backward.

Getting Things Done. David Allen's *Getting Things Done: the art of stress-free productivity* is "a gold mine of insights into strategies for how to have more energy, be more relaxed, with more clarity and presence in the moment with whatever you're doing and get a lot more accomplished with much

---

[31] J. Stockdale, *Thoughts of a Philosophical Fighter Pilot* (New York: Hoover Institution Press, 1995), 117.

less effort. If you're like me, you like getting things done and doing them well, and yet you also want to savor life in ways that seem increasingly elusive, if not downright impossible, if you're working too hard. This doesn't have to be an either-or proposition. It is possible to be effectively doing while you're delightfully being, in your ordinary workaday world."[32]

Allen's philosophy and methods changed how I approach both my personal and professional life. I took his advice to heart, followed his instructions carefully during a ten-day reordering of my life, and have benefited for years now in ways too numerous to catalog. The way I characterize the result of putting Allen's methods into action in my life is "mental freedom." He repeats, "The mind is to think about things, not of them."

My mind was decluttered so significantly following a reorganization that my head felt physically lighter. In short order, I found my mind a place of peaceful, open space instead of a hoarder's cram shack. After leaving my first tour of active-duty military service, I worked for Franklin Covey, the renowned time management folks. Allen's approach is explicitly *not* time management. "It is a coherent system of behavior and tools that functions at the level where work actually happens – on the ground – completing the smallest of open details in the context of the big picture."

---

[32] D. Allen, *Gettings Things Done: The Art of Stress-Free Productivity* (New York: Penguin Books, 2015), xxv.

He says, prophetically, that "a new practice creates a new reality." He advocates a bottom-up approach. To summarize, you handle the day-to-day first, capture and process everything, create a system you trust, know what to do next, free head space for big ideas, then start to look up. He wrote, "Your ability to generate power is directly proportional to your ability to relax." Hence, all else being equal, the most relaxed fighter wins.

Another crucial element of Allen's philosophy is the managing of commitments. Internal commitments are of utmost importance. Regardless of the scope (from changing a lightbulb to ending world hunger), committing to anything creates what Allen calls an "open loop." In essence, I've made a promise. All promises carry equal weight in our minds. Stress is created by the collision of unkept promises demanding immediate attention.

Allen's methods enable appropriate prioritization and sequencing of action, relieving the perpetual mental bombardment of open loops. The organization of "everything" allows me to categorize my open loops by deciding whether to "Do, Delegate, Defer, or Discard" them. Then I can begin to address my commitments effectively and efficiently. The process delivers on its promise to unleash creativity, energy, focus, and inspiration. Allen says that my sense of anxiety, stress, and guilt don't come from having too much to do or from being overwhelmed. "It is the result of breaking agreements with ourselves. These are the symptoms of disintegrated self-trust ... which we project also onto those with whom we work and live." We must create a new habit to reintegrate self-trust.

Through discipline, the learned skill of decision-making, and the creation of "a cognitive behavior pattern of 'knowledge-work-athletics'" I can "effectively do and delightfully be" in my ordinary world. If you recall the System 1 and System 2 thinking functions, Allen's approach creates freedom in System 2, liberating finite resources from the incessant churning of open loops. In this way, it effectively makes us smarter. A depleted System 2 is simply not as sharp as an alert, undertaxed System 2. Time is our most valuable commodity. How we spend it is our choice. Once spent we can never earn more. I must decide and act to facilitate the ambient tenor that I desire in my days. *Getting Things Done* is a profound methodology and, as Allen says, "A way is better than no way."

On The Playbook and the Rules. Universal laws are cold and without judgment (gravity, tornadoes, and electricity). Human laws codify the human social contract. The earliest known laws were published by the Sumerians around 2,000 years BCE. A few hundred years later, the well-known Code of Hammurabi, the sixth Amorite king of Old Babylon, consisted of 282 laws governing economics and family, criminal, and civil law. The most famous of these laws was "an eye for an eye and a tooth for a tooth." This law intended to govern retaliation in the event of a misdeed, to limit it to a punishment or cost commensurate with the crime.

Ironically, Hammurabi's Code meted out the death penalty liberally, for 25 offenses including adultery, taking a slave without a contract, perjury, kidnapping, or theft. The penalty was not delivered humanely, and it was not rendered equally across socio-economic strata. The death penalty involved gruesome suffering like being impaled, burned alive, crucified, or stoned. The "eye for an eye" law appears to have been treated subjectively. Law 53 stated that "if anyone be too lazy to keep his dam in proper condition, and if the dam then break and all the fields get flooded, then whoever let the dam break shall be sold for money (enslaved) and the money shall replace the crops which he caused to be ruined." Government-subsidized laziness was not woven into the tapestry of Babylonian life.

About 3,500 years ago (scholars' debate), Moses descended from Mount Sinai with the 10 Commandments. In historical context, it is important to recognize that Moses established the first monotheistic religion. As such, the first four commandments address religious requirements, the first being "Thou shalt have no other gods before me." The last six commandments, honor your father and mother, don't kill, commit adultery, lie, steal, or covet, apply to peaceful societal co-existence in a tribal environment. Though the results of violating a commandment are explicated elsewhere, the 10 Commandments themselves do not include punishments. Jesus later simplified these 10 commandments into two, captured in the book of Matthew. "You must love the Lord your God with all your heart, all your soul, and all your mind. This is the first and greatest commandment. A second is equally important: Love your neighbor as yourself. The entire law and all the demands of the prophets are based on these two commandments." Love transcends law by making it irrelevant. Laws are for haters. Peaceful coexistence requires that we make collective agreements regarding how we will behave toward one another.

Grappling with a clear definition of "good", as in "good person", requires an understanding of how humans have related forever. In <u>Tribe</u>, Sebastian Junger, journalist, author, and filmmaker, writes about human solidarity and the communal requirements that each of us must take responsibility for each other, muster courage, and sacrifice for the common good if we are to experience meaning in life.

Humans most often find meaning through connection with each other, through *belonging*, and in our soft Western affluence, it is too often only severe hardship that produces solidarity from necessity. "Humans don't mind hardship, in fact they thrive on it; what they mind is not feeling necessary. Modern society has perfected the art of making people not feel necessary."[33] Junger points out that "mental health issues refuse to decline with growing wealth" because "modern society seems to emphasize extrinsic values over intrinsic ones."[34] This constitutes a well-known fallacy where short-term gain obfuscates long-term costs. In modern Western society, systemic forces

---

[33] S. Junger, *Tribe: On Homecoming and Belonging* (New York: Harper Collins, 2016), xxi.
[34] Ibid., 22.

prioritize capital consumption over what Junger describes as "something called self-determination theory", in which the three basic human needs for contentment are simply feelings of competence, authenticity, and connection. In war and disaster, topics that Junger has experienced and written about extensively, individuals are more apt to experience connection than in times of plenty and ease.

Hard times level the playing field. Our differences dissolve during existential crisis and what we share unites us in survival. Individuals are judged by what they can contribute to the common good, irrespective of economic status or political, religious, or racial differences. In combat, everyone is the color "green." Nothing matters but what an individual brings to the fight and each is judged based on his or her competence, reliability, and unselfishness. In ancient tribal fashion, new military members are initiated first into the force and then into their respective units via specific rites of passage. During wartime, participation in combat marks another rite of passage.

In military ranks during America's "long war" against terror, there were those who had deployed to combat and those who had not. For many, this rite became so important that a soldier would volunteer for any combat deployment that he or she could join. Failure to participate directly in the war alongside brothers and sisters in uniform directly undermined feelings of competence, authenticity, and connection. Junger eloquently explains what I and many combat veterans feel when they retrospectively "miss" combat and wish they could go back.

He also recounts the same sentiments from survivors of other catastrophic situations. What a combat veteran misses is not the gore of war, but the deep belonging and sense of purpose.

A man remembers who he *was* during that time. Remember that human will and purpose reside in the heart as the center of our being. To experience the feeling of being a good (authentic) human, I must know what is required of me, have confidence in my ability to carry it out, and do so within the context of a higher purpose, that of self-sacrificial support for my tribe, which Junger describes most simply as the people I will feed and defend. I deeply desire to be a man who feeds and defends. In *Man's Search for Meaning,*

Viktor Frankl proposes that the "meaning of life" is not a single answer to an eternal question but is the answer at any moment as to why I got out of bed this morning or, more bluntly, why I wouldn't kill myself. Junger posits a similar theme by asking "What would I die for?" The descendent question I ask is "What will I live for?" The answers to questions like these are rarely selfishly focused, rather are centered around those people in my life for whom I want to be here, to provide for and protect, and to not let down.

Of course, a continually expanding body of laws, impenetrable by sheer volume and complexity, is also a control measure wielded by central governments (e.g., IRS tax codes). That's why The Sage boils it down to two things that anyone can remember and places the responsibility on the individual. Codes of conduct, laws, and societal rules seek to preserve the most elemental of human needs by protecting those of goodwill against those who selfishly seek gain at the detriment of the collective. We are made for each other. Modern existential angst is a direct result of losing sight of this. The blood of our ancestors cries from the ground that we remember and that we do not forget.

On Throwing Out the Playbook. Sometimes you do something bad because, if you don't, something worse will happen. Most are familiar with the distinction between the "letter" and the "spirit" of the law. Rules are created with a behavioral intent in mind, either to encourage or prohibit specific behavior in a known context. We also know that following the rules does not by itself constitute moral uprightness.

Good citizens break laws as often as bad citizens obey them. If I approach a stop sign on a deserted road, the letter of the law dictates that I come to a complete stop before entering the intersection. The law exists, in spirit, to prevent vehicle collisions in the intersection. For my safety, even on a deserted road, I will slow at intersections to ensure that no other vehicles are approaching. If I don't fully stop at the sign, I've broken the letter of the law while preserving the spirit of it. I adhere to its intent – prevent collisions – while ignoring its prescriptions, some of which are contextually irrelevant on an empty series of roads.

Carrying this bucket of logic up the hill, I conclude that laws of themselves, whether abided or broken, are insufficient markers to determine goodness or rightness in the heart of an individual. This is the heart of Jesus' parable about washing the cup. If you wash the inside of the cup the outside is made clean. If my heart and my honor are clean, I will naturally do more than follow laws, I will fulfill them by rendering them irrelevant. On the path to becoming who you would be, this principle is central.

Professionally, the principle also holds. My military experience began with an introduction to and study of what Stockdale referred to as the "playbook." From codes of conduct to tactics, young soldiers learn the what, why, and how of military service. Almost everything is spelled out and reduced to the lowest common denominator. A deep and working knowledge of the playbook is essential. For leaders, they must know it well enough to know when to make decisions and order actions beyond the prescriptions of doctrine.

In some cases, a leader must order that something "bad" be done (i.e., bend or break a rule) to prevent something worse from happening. It is only knowledge of the letter *and* spirit of the law that enables a leader to effectively make such calls. He or she must also have the courage to accept the consequences of such a decision. The bureaucracy of the military chain of command, too often politically pressured, may care more that the leader broke the rule than they do about the lives or the equipment that the leader saved by breaking it.

Krav Maga. I was introduced to Krav Maga while on active-duty military service. Our group regularly employed a South African hand-to-hand combat instructor to teach us how to fight. Among the many styles he had mastered, our instructor included techniques from Krav Maga. Later, in a strip mall studio near my home, I studied Krav at least three days per week for over a year.

Though I never reached what I would consider functional proficiency, i.e., I was in Krav Maga but Krav Maga was not yet embodied in me, the simplicity and effectiveness of the techniques were powerful. My mindset shifted from defeating an attacker to protecting myself. I'm not here to "win"; I'm here to survive. If I don't survive, I'll never "win" anything again. My mind and body began to learn how to repel malevolent forces to preserve the sanctity of my existence and my personal autonomy. This is a life principle.

The Israeli close combat and hand-to-hand fighting style Krav Maga began with Emerich "Imi" Lichtenfeld (Sde-Or). The two Hebrew words translate as "struggle" or "combat" and "contact" respectively. Imi was born in Czechoslovakia in 1910. His father was part of a professional circus troupe and trained extensively in wrestling, boxing, mixed-skill fighting, and fitness. Later, Imi's father founded a wrestling club and gym where Imi became a world-class gymnast, ballet dancer, and champion in judo, wrestling, and ballroom dancing.

In 1935 Imi traveled to Palestine to compete in the Jewish Maccabi sports convention with a team of wrestlers. He fractured a rib during training and could not compete. This led to Imi's fundamental training philosophy, "*Don't get hurt.*" He concluded that only absolute necessity justifies a "win at all costs" mindset. From these tenets Imi later created Krav Maga's training approach.

Escalating anti-Semitic Nazi violence in Czechoslovakia motivated Imi to organize a group of young Jews to protect his community. Imi quickly learned the difference between organized martial competitions and street fighting. Imi's leadership and "insurgency" efforts against the Nazis made him a Nazi target. In 1940, he boarded a boat bound for Palestine to escape the fascists' systematic Jewish extermination campaign. Following a perilous journey, the boat's engine failed and Imi, along with three others, rowed a lifeboat for three days until a British airplane spotted them and a British warship rescued them. Imi enlisted in the British-supervised Free Czech Legion and, after exemplary military service, was released following the Afrika Korp's defeat at El Alamain in 1942. Imi was allowed to remain in British-ruled Palestine.

Imi began training elite Israeli military forces and marine fighting units. He became the principal authority in close-quarters combat training for the Israeli Defense Forces (IDF). Working with soldiers of all types, physical capabilities, fitness levels, and ages from young to old, he developed a system that could be learned quickly and implemented effectively by "anyone", independent of physical strength or expertise in combatives. Imi incorporated techniques to evolve with modern threats and myriad combatant weaponry.[35]

---

[35] Kahn, Krav Maga History [summarized]. www.isrealikrav.com

The objective of Krav Maga's combination of defensive and offensive actions and the speed and aggression with which they are employed is not to utterly defeat an opponent but to neutralize them so that the Krav practitioner can avoid injury, survive, and disengage as quickly as possible. *Don't get hurt and live to fight another day.* Risks increase as the practitioner encounters multiple attackers, for which Krav Maga students train extensively, requiring rapid, natural movements and countermovements to address threats quickly so that the practitioner can disengage and move to safety.

Nassim N. Taleb's investment philosophy captures the same principle of preventing ruin in Antifragile. Guard against mortal wounds, act decisively and avoid unnecessary risks that could result in annihilation. If you can go big without the risk of obliteration, consider it if the payoff is substantial. In a fight, if I've successfully neutralized an opponent and have an opportunity to either deliver the "knockout blow" or escape, I must weigh all factors. If the final (but unnecessary) blow will open me to another attacker driving a knife between my ribs, I don't do it. It's not an emotional decision, as much as the judge in me wants my attacker to pay for his sins. I must discern when enough is enough.

Most of our endeavors in life do not carry the high stakes of life and death, or wealth versus destitution. But in aggregate, the thousands of decisions we make result in the lives we live and the beings we become. As Pareto, Via Negativa, Antifragile, and "less is more" teach us, "don't get hurt." Eliminate or prevent the threats (i.e., habits, laziness, influences, substances) that are or have the potential to be the most detrimental. Remember, most good is the absence of bad.

Stress is Good. In the U.S., the last generation has seen dramatic increases in anxiety-related conditions and medications, especially among teens and young adults. The overwhelming existential angst of modern man, as depicted in Munch's 1893 painting, "The Scream", appears now to have become a prevalent "baseline normal" for many in Western society. (Figure 1) The last century of progress has not been kind to our nervous systems. The "gust of melancholy" that Munch cited as the impetus for the painting sounds familiar.

The maelstrom of noise and information, coupled with a sudden onset of aimlessness and meaninglessness, culminates in a paralyzing sense of *disconnected suffering*. A primal scream seems an appropriate response. Stress management has taken the lead over time management as a priority for sustainable production. I use p*roduction* intentionally because much of our value as individuals in Western society is based solely on our ability to produce. We keep score by the perpetual accrual of material possessions, but the individual's value, or the social capital earned, is based on productivity, from which quantifiable material gain serves as a marker. Production is not bad. The U.S. cultural focus on forward progress has ushered the entire world into a new reality. The lowest standard of living for almost all in capitalistic societies far exceeds ancient luxury standards. The royalty of old did not have running water or climate control in their castles.

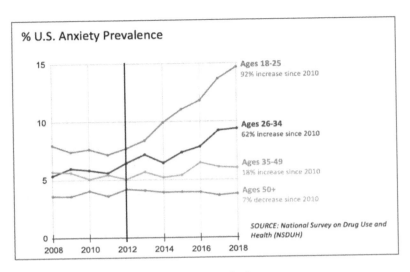

(Figure 1)[36]

In Mihaly Csikszentmihalyi's seminal best-seller *Flow*, the author examines moments of "optimal experience" – the *flow state* – where "people are so involved in an activity that nothing else seems to matter; the experience itself is so enjoyable that people will do it even at great cost, for the sheer sake of doing it."[37] The flow state is characterized by a satisfied feeling, *happiness*, and depends entirely on our internal interpretation of outside events, not by the nature of external events themselves. Perhaps happiness *is* simply acceptance of and full participation in "what happens." *Amor Fati*. Csikszentmihalyi quotes Viktor Frankl, "Don't aim at success—the more you aim at it and make it a target, the more you are going to miss it. For success, like happiness, cannot be pursued; it must ensue . . . as the

---

36 Source: https://www.afterbabel.com/
37 M. Csikszentmihalyi, *Flow* (New York: Harper, 1990), 4.

unintended side-effect of one's personal dedication to a course greater than oneself."[38]

Again, we see that the principle of contribution to the Common Good, a higher calling, God, or a purpose greater than oneself is vital to happiness, and, in the context of Csikszentmihalyi's studies, to optimal experience. Additionally, the author points out that self-improvement in one or more areas of a person's life does not equate to increased happiness. When viewed as a product, or an output (e.g., goal, end state, top rung, metric), the process becomes a means to an end. The mindset difference between process (the daily grind) versus product (my idealized self) is the difference between taking a highway or the scenic route. In either case, the next destination is known, but the travel to it highlights completely different experiences. When I take the highway, my mindset is one of efficiency, speed, and directness. I keep the destination in mind and think, "I'll be happy when I arrive. Vacation starts then."

Conversely, if I load my car with the mindset that my vacation has already started and choose the scenic route, I do so intentionally to experience the travel, come what may. I choose to be happy now by experiencing what happens along the way. Csikszentmihalyi unpacks how consciousness works and methods to control it to equip the reader with tools to shape their perception, to bring *"order in consciousness."*[39] The reader is given the power to

---

[38] Ibid., 2.
[39] Ibid., 6.

choose what their lives will be like not by changing their life but by seeing it anew. *My life is exactly what I think it is.* In such efforts, the struggle itself is the place from which most derive the greatest joy. Again, the obstacle does not impede the way but is the way. Struggling, even failure, is the point.

You need stress to perform your best. Many versions of the anxiety/performance curve depict the value of optimal levels of stress for peak performance. (Figure 2) Plotted along a bell curve, too little stress results in boredom, complacency, and rote actions. As you rise toward the peak of the curve, between 5-6 of 10, performance and creative energy peak as well. On the back side of the curve, from 6-10, performance goes back down proportional to rising levels of stress. Too little stress results in lackluster performance and too much stress results in increasing dysfunction. At either tail end, a level 0 stress (none) is as dangerous to holistic health as a level 10 (unmanageable and overwhelming). The middle is the sweet spot.

It is important to assess where you reside on the curve. You may experience different stress levels in different areas of your life. Reduce stress in areas where it is too high (e.g., employ the *Getting Things Done* methodology) and increase it in areas where it is too low (learn something new). In many cases, *reordering* is an effective way to reduce stress. A healthy dose of added stress can be found in a variety of ways, from learning something new to rechanneling unresolved emotional energy into creative effort.

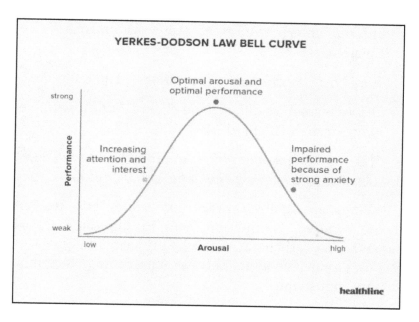

(Figure 2)

The human body doesn't make a distinction between "healthy" and "unhealthy" stress, so it's not necessary to invest too much time parsing that out. Think simply in terms of overall volume in specific areas, and the results, and decide which pedal needs to be pressed, either gas or brake.

The Reframe. On mindset and reframing your reality.

"Don't worry about tomorrow; each day has enough trouble of its own." -The Sage

"What really frightens and dismays us is not external events themselves, but the way in which we think about them. It's not things that disturb us,

but our interpretation of their significance." -Epictetus

"Our life is the creation of our mind." -The Buddha

"There is nothing either good or bad, but thinking makes it so." -The Bard

"The mind is its own place, and in itself can make a heaven of a hell, a hell of a heaven." -Milton

Feelings are almost always *compelling* but are not always *reliable*. I think of them in the same way I remember a charismatic and lushy bridesmaid I once met at a wedding reception. She was compelling, certainly. Reliable, not so much.

Imagine that you are riding an elephant. It's easier if you've ridden an elephant, but not to worry. Picture yourself straddling a rowboat that has been turned belly up on a swaying sea swell. It feels something like that. My conscious, rational mind is the rider on the elephant. It has the reigns. Everything else in my mind, my emotional being and my primal brain, is the elephant. It's a ton. The elephant is more powerful than the rider, naturally, and the idea of total control over it is delusional. But the rider can reframe what the elephant "sees" and influence its behavior. The rider can train the elephant. Or the rider can engage in the cognitive distortion of interpreting reality in ways that are consistent with the elephant's feelings and behavior, acting as a lawyer and press secretary to the elephant, warping reality instead of investigating the truth. *(I heard this analogy used once but did not know to whom to attribute it. Research revealed that Jonathan Haidt, NYU psychologist, may have been the first to present this analogy, though I am unfamiliar with his work. Any misrepresentation of his analogy is unintentional.)*

Delusion, histrionics, and anxiety are the result of disproportional thinking. The Stoics (and others) provide a visual analogy to picture appropriate emotional responses to events. Imagine a placid pond. If you toss a pebble into it, there is a small *kerplunk* and little concentric ripples that fan out from the center. The ripples don't last long and dissipate quickly. There is little energy in them. When you throw a brick into the pond there is a big splash that produces breaking waves. They contain substantial energy, and it may require a few minutes before the pond returns to glass. The pond is your mind.

The pebbles and bricks are events. The ripples or waves are your emotional response. Emotions are natural. Things happen and we feel them. Emotions themselves are not shortcomings. It is the degree to which we express them in response to the world that determines healthy function. The vital effort is learning to respond appropriately to events based on their relevant weight. When a pebble drops into my pond and my elephant shrieks and begins to stampede, as the rider I must reframe the event to restore sanity.

Another seductive mental distortion is to use myself as the baseline "normal" for comparative external judgments. If you drive faster than me, you're a maniac. If you drive slower than me, you're an idiot. If you're fatter than me, you're lazy. If you're fitter than me, you're obsessive. God did not put me on this planet to be judge, jury, and executioner for his children. In psychological circles, the *mean* variable can be a valuable marker to indicate the relative health of an individual. The mean is established scientifically by observing thousands or millions of humans. I am not the mean variable. Nor are you. At the poles of the distribution, the margins, live those with psychological disorders.

The soldier who is *always* afraid is a coward, a capital offense punishable by death. The soldier who is *never* afraid is psychotic. Both are a danger to themselves and others. Most of us exist somewhere in the middle and are sometimes this and sometimes that. My position along any number of continuums is not a scientific marker by which to effectively judge others, nor is it an infallible point of reference for the determination of reality. To learn to live with myself I must get over myself.

When I start my car and the stereo system startles me because it's at level 44, I turn it down in shock. The last time I was behind the wheel I was jamming! It wasn't too loud then, but it is now. If no music turns on, I may think I have a technology issue, that something isn't pairing correctly. It's too quiet. How I experience and evaluate volume is *contextual*. Shortcomings are normal, healthy functions that fail to reach appropriate levels of expression – they're too quiet, and under-expressed. Character disorders are normal, healthy functions that exceed appropriate levels of expression – they're too loud and over-expressed. My emotional orchestra has a mixing board with tone, pitch, distortion, and volume knobs. I can turn it down or turn it up. I can adjust and learn to live between the poles. I can become a willing participant in life, neither the center of attention nor sulking in the corner, who appropriately responds to life and enjoys the ride.

Jocko Willink tells a story that is familiar to many veterans of foreign wars. When you're in combat, it's the only thing that matters. It is consuming. You put everything else in your life on the back burner. After sustained combat in one of the rowdiest towns in Iraq, Jocko was assigned to a role where he did a lot of paperwork. He recalls feeling like the paperwork didn't matter and was frustrated that he had to do it. From war hero to desk jockey. Paperwork feels meaningless if your mind is still in combat. He realized that piles of paperwork don't matter in the context of gunfights, but that he was no longer in a gunfight.

When you come home, everything seems trivial, excessive, bureaucratic, and soft. You're gone for six months or a year and return to find that the entire population has become self-absorbed, sniveling clods complaining that they only got two pumps of syrup in their coffee instead of three and now their entire day is ruined. The truth is, the population has not changed, it's that I have not come home yet. In my head and my heart, I'm still *over there*. But what matters is what I'm doing *now*. Combat matters to those still in the fight. It's always the most important thing to those doing it. Once I come home, the battles being fought *right now* don't "matter" to me anymore, they are no longer my focus, in the sense that I now have been assigned a task that is important within its context. If my job is to do paperwork, the paperwork is important. Though I will always *care* that my brothers and sisters are in harm's way and may find myself in a position where I support their efforts from home station, what I'm doing today is the most important thing. I must be where I am.

There is value in working through things and getting to the bottom of your "issues", but sometimes you just need to get over them. You're not there anymore (wherever there is), you're here (wherever you are now). If a bully beat you up when you were seven and you're now 33 and still stewing about it, it's time to grow up. Either track that guy down and thrash him (it won't make you feel better) or let it go and drive on. You're not that kid anymore. There's work to do. Turn on some loud music, load a heavy bar, and handle it. Everything does not always have to be a life lesson. Most of the time, there's simply stuff that needs doing and you need to do it. Focus on your five-meter targets. Do the next right thing. Leave your ego at the door.

Resistance Creates Pain. If I do not think that human existence is comprised chiefly of suffering, I have read too little of history. Scratching survival from an indifferent earth is no mean feat. Life will be hard. The wisdom of the thinkers encourages us to not manufacture additional misery. When I judge "what happens" negatively, I experience negative emotions. Many of us become conditioned to view the world through a negative lens by default. As a result, I can move through my day perpetually passing quiet judgment, writing scathing mental narratives, and simmering in a hot bath of negative emotions. In this condition, life sucks. It's miserable. Thankfully, I have a choice.

Our minds are a tool that we intentionally or unwittingly employ to create our reality. We create pain by resisting what already exists, standing in opposition to reality, and wishing it were different. Acceptance of reality enables me to live life on its terms, a mindset shift equivalent to the difference between swimming up a stream or floating down it. Our memories are useful, in the evolutionary sense, as an instrument to keep us from repeating mistakes that will get us killed. We have few or no thoughts that do not have as their descendants a family of emotions.

These are single-parent families, with either Love or Fear acting as mother and father to their corresponding offspring. As a system, our minds conjure our memories programmatically, with an unbiased code that pulls them with existing connections. Some modern therapies, e.g., Eye Movement Desensitization and Reprocessing (EMDR), seek to "reprogram" the emotional offspring of painful memories. It has been used successfully to treat memories of trauma by reassociating the memory of the events with positive emotions.

Another treatment protocol is Cognitive Behavioral Therapy (CBT). Based on a cyclical model where core beliefs produce dysfunctional assumptions that result in automatic negative thoughts, CBT talk therapy employs tools to deconstruct problems into smaller, more manageable parts. It brings awareness to patterns of inaccurate, problematic, or negative thinking and uncovers the connection between thinking and behavior. CBT is an archaeological dig to unearth source beliefs and central ideas that govern the way I view myself and the world. These beliefs are the raw materials from which I manufacture what I think and feel about what happens and, accordingly, how I behave.

My experience has been that understanding my core belief systems is crucial to providing context for how I think and feel, but awareness does not result in behavioral change. An understanding coupled with intentional corrective or corrected action, however, is a powerful combination. Once I know how my central beliefs influence my perception of reality and why I think and feel the way I do, I can purposefully change my behavior to align with what I truly believe. I can act my way into a new pattern of thinking. I can also change my beliefs through the logical application of knowledge. If my high school girlfriend cheated on me, I may have unconsciously decided, and written into my core belief system, that "all women are liars."

Unaware, this belief taints or dooms future relationships. I bring to every potential partner a suitcase full of premeditated verdicts and corresponding emotions that I am certain to act out on the stage of our relationship. Consciously, I wonder why it never works out. Subconsciously, I treated her like a liar from the moment I met her. The shortest route to a healthier outlook is both understanding my core beliefs and modifying behavior or accruing knowledge intentionally as it relates to a *specific* belief. The value of precision in this endeavor cannot be overstated. Contending with a single belief at a time provides enough challenge.

Quantum Physics consists of analyzing things that are experienced in life, in various forms, and tracing them back to their origin, from which they were derived, which in any case is energy. It is the study of subatomic particles: photons, leptons, electrons, neutrons, and quarks. E=MC2 or energy = everything. Subatomic particles are pure energy. It's staggering to think of the energy contained in an object with the mass of a small coin traveling at the speed of light squared. Neils Bohr changed Einstein's theory, stating something like energy doesn't exist as particles, but in waveform. Everything breaks down from the cosmos: universe—galaxy—earth—individuals—organ systems—cells—molecules—atoms—subatomic particles—energy.

The Secret (where it gets weird): subatomic particles (waves) being studied by scientists responded to, transmuted, and appeared as particles (solid objects) *based on the individual thought of the scientist who was studying it*. The scientist's mode of thinking *determined the form* of the particles. Anything and everything that exists in our world once existed as a wave (spiritual) and through individual observation and expectation was transformed into a particle (made physical) based only on what they *thought* and *believed* it would appear as. Modern-day quantum physics fully explains that your thoughts are the things that group to collapse energy packets, change those thoughts from a probability into physical matter in each place and time, and create your life experience physically, emotionally, relationally, financially (materially), and spiritually.[40]

Quantum Entanglement. When subatomic particles are divided, they can communicate via vibration. Communication is received from one half to the other instantaneously, regardless of how far apart they are. Their communication is not subject to space and time. Energy doesn't need to travel because all energy is interconnected. Your beliefs broadcast outward into the infinite field of wave energy and vibrate at a harmonious frequency to shape waves into particles and shape your life experience (your physical world). Everything is an interconnected system of systems. How you think (and why) matters. How you act matters even more. We create and we destroy in this way.

"All matter originates and exists only by virtue of a force . . . we must assume behind this force the existence of a conscious and Intelligent Mind. The Mind is the matrix of all matter." –Max Planck

Dr. Harry Tiebout, a psychologist who studied members of Alcoholics Anonymous, published a paper in 1949 to establish *surrender* as a psychic event in the therapeutic process. Dr. Tiebout described "submission" as conscious acceptance of reality, but subconscious rejection. "I'll accept it now, but there will come a day..."[41] He defined

---

[40] www.iempowerself.com
[41] H. Tiebout, *The Collected Writings* (New York: Hazeldon, 1999), .22.

"surrender" as acceptance of reality on a subconscious level. Following *surrender*, an individual ceases to resist reality. The observed results were relaxation, freedom from strain and internal conflict, and the clearing of battle rubble. Tiebout measured the degree of acceptance of reality (subconscious) in direct proportion to the degree of ensuing relaxation following the event. He stated that it is "the moment when the unconscious forces of defiance and grandiosity actually cease to function effectively", captured in the sentiment that, "From that time on, things have been different."[42]

The blocks to acceptance are defiance and grandiosity. If you recall the emergence of consciousness and a toddler's defiant statements of sovereignty, *defiance* is my perpetual insistence on my individuality. Respecting the need for change in my life, defiance blocks my ability to see that I am subject to the same laws of nature as every other human being. I insist that I'm different and a special case. I wield defiance by rejecting reality, particularly when it's obvious, and respond to truth with a stubborn but toothless "that's not true." Until I become open to the possibility that maybe there are some truths I need to face about myself whether I like them or not, change is impossible. Surrender can be defined "as a state in which there is a persisting capacity to accept reality."[43]

The toddler portion of my psyche, the *infantile ego*, suffers also from visions of grandeur. Grandiosity

---

[42] Ibid., 23.
[43] Ibid.

manifests itself as self-deification (omnipotence: I know everything), demands gratification, interprets frustration as rejection or a lack of love, and believes that there is nothing it cannot control.

Tiebout categorized his patients who surrendered in three ways: 1) A single surrender event is all that is needed, followed by forever remaining immersed in the program, attending meetings, and following the program diligently; 2) Surrender is the beginning of continued growth and maturation; patients grow out of their condition(s); and, 3) "Selective Surrender", when a patient surrenders in one area (alcohol cessation) and simply carries on unchanged otherwise.

At the heart of surrender is humility. Stephan W. Gilbert, a retired professor from the University of Guadalajara, in a paper titled *Etymologies of Humor: Reflections on the Humus Pile*, digs into the etymology of humor in a trio of words sharing a common root – "human", "humility", and "humor." (also in Kurtz & Ketcham).

From the Latin *humus*, "a careful combination of rotting vegetable matter", comes the root for all three words. The etymological linkage to humility is evident but how is it humorous, i.e., why is it funny? Humor is the juxtaposition of the incongruent. Humus represents not only death but also rebirth. As higher forms are degraded and reduced to elements, the loss is felt but the energy transfers to new life. The contrast of death and rebirth, the most sublime of incongruent juxtapositions, results in laughter, the deepest and most human of laughter, that which conjures and channels the divine.

"We laugh *from* below, in allowing the degrading power of the lower bodily material stratum its full force, accepting it for what it is, democratic, final, and irrevocable...And the laughter is divine...Divine laughter is helpless laughter. The recognition that all social constructions are but frail, weak, and finally ineffectual in the face of the inevitable regenerative force and movement of the material life force, located ridiculously (ridiculous only when you think about it) in the lower bodily stratum, calls forth an irrepressible belly laugh." (Gilbert)

This is the Cosmic Joke. Humility constitutes "realignment with the force for life that laughs at the meager attempts of human authority to impose its own order on things." To be human means to be of the earth, a composition of dirt and minerals, what Marcus Aurelius called "spirits carrying corpses." I take myself quite seriously until I recognize where I fit into the natural order. I stomp around, petulant and resistant, until I accept my humble beginnings and my inevitable end. It dawns on me like a punch line and it's divinely hilarious. Humility is not thinking less of yourself, it's thinking of yourself less.

Tell the truth. Nietzsche said, "The strength of a person's spirit would then be measured by how much 'truth' he could tolerate, or more precisely, to what extent he needs to have it diluted, disguised, sweetened, muted, falsified."

4 – *Commitment (Disciplined Doing)*

One thing is vital to growth: 100% honesty. It's a tall order and, until scrutinized, we often don't realize the extent to which we diminish, mince, soften, or avoid honesty in everyday language. As I don't get from others (or myself) what I expect, I get what I tolerate, I also cannot expect honesty when I am unwilling to provide it. If my spouse asks me if her jeans make her look fat, I want to be the one person she can count on to give it to her straight. There's an idea that a person can't lie to themselves.

If you must ask if your jeans make you look fat, you already know the answer. Regardless of what my mind tells me, my heart – my center – always knows the truth. I observe a proportional relationship between the mental gymnastics required to spin a self-delusion and the degree of the lie. The greater the departure from truth, the more voluminous and demanding the mental machinations.

Bluster implies distortion and deception. A leader isn't helpful when he or she sugarcoats failure, lack of skill, poor performance, blame, slippery behavior, or less than a person's best. If I am to effectively lead myself, I must be willing to traffic in truth, "the brutal facts of my current reality." (Stockdale) I lie to you because I think you can't handle the truth. I attempt to lie to myself because I'm afraid to square up to the truth. I must learn to talk in straight lines, not in circles. I must expose myself to and build a tolerance to unvarnished, undiluted, and unmitigated truths about myself. The extent to which I can handle truth enables me to speak it to others. As gossip is a polite form of murder, a man who can "dish it out but can't take it" is a double-minded hypocrite and exposed by the degree of his dishing.

The Fool and the Riddle. A classic device in literature, theater in particular, is the character of the fool (court jester) who delivers wisdom at crucial moments. Paradoxically, it is the fool who knows the answers to the riddles. Regrettably, the tragic protagonist rarely attends to the fool's musings and suffers, nonetheless. The Sage's parables often employed paradox to depict non-obvious realities about the nature of the universe. Unless you become a little child (are reborn – a literal "impossibility"), you may not enter the Kingdom of the Heavens, or you must lose your life to find it.

In everyday language, the oxymoron captures incongruous words in a phrase, like "jumbo shrimp" or "virtual reality." In Greek, *oxy* means sharp and *moros* means dumb. A paradox is, simply, a self-contradictory statement. Oxford Dictionary defines it as a seemingly absurd or self-contradictory statement or proposition that when investigated or explained may prove to be well-founded or true.

Examples are the *information paradox*, which observes the conflicts between quantum mechanics and the general theory of relativity, and the *irresistible force paradox*, which asks what happens when an unstoppable force meets an immovable object, as when the unstoppable bullet strikes the impenetrable wall or the spear that can pierce anything hits the shield that is un-pierceable. The "core paradox that underlies spirituality is the haunting sense of incompleteness, of being somehow *unfinished*, that comes from the reality of living on this earth as part and yet also not-part of it."[44] From incompleteness, brokenness, and imperfection we yearn for completion, wholeness, and perfection. These desires are and will remain unfulfilled, as this great paradox defines what it means to be "humanly imperfect." "Paradox and ambiguity reside at the heart of the human condition."[45]

The primary struggle with paradox is not the solving of the riddle (if God is all-powerful, can he create a rock so big that He can't pick it up?), but in the acceptance of it as an enduring quality of human life and a fine sense of what to take literally and what figuratively. To some questions, I must resolve myself to never receive answers. How is my life never enough but somehow always enough? Why must I learn to tell myself "No" so that I can say "Yes" to what I want from life? How can giving up everything I have result in getting everything that I ever wanted? Why does freedom require self-slavery to discipline?

How is it that embracing, honoring, and making space for the dark places of my shadow is the surest way to illuminate who I am and what it means to be me, to step into the light? The conundrums of paradox do not exist as puzzles for solving. Rather, instances of paradox mark the "best things in life", as Joseph Campbell said, which

---

[44] *The Spirituality of Imperfection: Storytelling And The Search For Meaning*, 19.
[45] Ibid, 38.

"cannot be told." The awe of our existence is punctuated by the ineffable, the inexplicable, and the incongruous.

To encounter a true paradox is to wonder. It is a call to pay attention. In the struggle to self-actualize, to improve, or to potentiate, the chief obstacle is self-obsession. The freedom we need most immediately is paradoxical freedom from self-preoccupation. "Sages and saints throughout the centuries have maintained that it is in this willingness to give up the self and give in to others that the road to human wholeness can be found. And for those who would give up 'self', the first step is to give up certainty."[46]

Monks fascinate me. I've always been drawn to the simplicity of their lives and their purity of heart. Equally intriguing are lawless motorcycle gangs. In either case, initiates are called to dispense with societal norms, a sacrifice made toward earning a brand of freedom, one spiritual and the other primal. A glorious tempest of a woman I love dearly tattooed the words "Saint" and "Sinner" on her hips, one on each side. The hip region is associated with the sacral chakra, an energetic center believed by some to house creative energy (and sexuality). It's also linked to how you relate to your emotions and the emotions of others.

In the hips, we are made and from the hips, we are born. The power of this energy both perpetuates and sustains human life. In raw form, energy is pure potential, neither creative nor destructive. Mother Nature is indifferent.

---

[46] Ibid., 39.

When it becomes kinetic, energy surges where the channels route it. Harnessing this energy, we reach the heights of creative power or the depths of destruction. Chuck C. said that electricity can light the room, fry your bacon, or fry your ass. Like God and nature, electricity isn't "mean" (intentionally hurtful) but it is dangerous. The dichotomy of the monk and the outlaw split my self-image. Presented were the poles of human existence, as I could conceive of it, as a one-or-the-other path.

Anything less than a commitment to an "all in" life felt mediocre or middling. I wanted it all. I didn't recognize the foolishness of such grandiosity for over two decades. The truth is that I'm not "good" enough to be a monk, nor am I "bad" enough to be an outlaw. Regardless, the electromagnetic pull of the poles endures and I am suspended between them. I am neither of those things and yet I am both. We are neither and we are both. This is another paradox of human existence. Being "both bound and free, both limited and unlimited" creates the ambient anxiety of humanity. I will forever tread the middle road between the divine and the mundane.[47] I am a saint and I am a sinner, dauntless and terrified, full of love and contempt, a truth-teller and a prevaricator, frantic and placid, both sage and idiot. Contained in each of us is the dark and light – the angel and the demon – of mythic proportions. What then?

Again, acceptance, surrender, abandonment. I can never fully be either of those. The Yin-Yang symbol contains a

[47] Ibid., 52.

spot of black on the white side and a spot of white on the black side. Chaos has a dose of order and order has a dose of chaos. The winding path between them is paradox-in-motion, the path of a human having a spiritual experience, or a spirit having a human experience, in a temporal world between worlds.

On the road to commitment, it is incumbent that we detach from grandiose visions. We must let go of outcomes, distance ourselves from unrealistic expectations, and live out the *process* intentionally with as little regard for the *product* as possible. There is never a final human product. A romantic version of this idea is that each human is an exquisite but unfinished poem being written by the Great Spirit, who writes, edits, and adds to, but never finishes. Simultaneously, we experience decay and rebirth. Part of me is dying and part of me is regenerating.

The knowledge that no matter how hard I try I will never achieve completeness in this life is a form of liberation. Disabused of perfectionism, I am freed to do my best and that suffices. A great sculptor was once asked how he created masterpieces. He answered that he observed the block of stone and chiseled away all that was *not* the sculpture. As you chip away all that is not your highest self, take comfort knowing that the sculpture you envision lives within and take heart, for you will forever be chipping, chiseling, and sanding toward that which *cannot be told*. Be patient and take it easy. The rewards for commitment are substantial and worth the wait.

Don't Waste the Gift. Steve Prefontaine, an Olympic runner in 1972, said, "To give anything less than your best is to sacrifice the gift." Despite what current political narratives would lead you to believe, having opportunity or talent isn't a sin. However, squandering talent or opportunity are sins.

Prefontaine also said something like, "Somebody may beat me, but they'll have to bleed to do it." Commitment looks a lot like that. Prefontaine had grit. We all are capable of something and, most likely, a lot of things. But we can't do *anything*, nor can we do *everything*. Sacrificing the gift is failing to do my best. If God gave me the life I have, it makes sense that I would want to repay him, possibly with interest. I must resist the urge to focus on what I am incapable of and choose instead to invest heavily in what I can do.

Showing up to life is the first step and a necessary one, but I must put my back into it. Whatever heat you have, bring it. If life was a gunfight, at the end of it you'd want to be holding a gun with a melted barrel, standing knee-deep in hand grenade pins and spent shell casings, smoking your last cigarette while you bleed out. Do your best.

When I am immature (at any age), I confuse irresponsibility with freedom. Freedom is not the unfettered expression of my desire or lawless misbehavior. True freedom requires a willingness to submit to universal laws and to grow through a period of un-freedom (discipline). Pay the price. Grace, forgiveness, and hospitality are gifts. Freedom is a reward, not a gift. The orthopraxy of earning freedom is learning to stay put and finish well, put skin in the game (tangible risk and reward), and execute consistently.

Don't Wear Clip-on Ties. Never attempt to look like something – be something. Be who you are while you chip away at becoming the person you want to be. That's not a suggestion to wear sweatpants to the next wedding you attend. But, if you don't know how to tie a necktie, and you are over the age of 12, you have two choices: 1) learn how to tie a necktie, or 2) don't wear a tie. Wearing a clip-on necktie is not wearing a tie, it's *pretending* to wear a tie or it's wearing a *pretend* tie. Don't do that. People can respect a man who says, "I don't wear ties, not even to weddings." The man who wears a legitimate necktie goes unnoticed because it's status quo. The man wearing the clip-on tie skylines himself as possibly any of numerous undesirable characterizations: lazy, unsophisticated, oblivious, immature, or ridiculous. Be a dude who wears ties or doesn't.

Don't wear a pretend tie. Moreover, don't eat things pretending to be other things. I like bread. When I'm monitoring carbohydrate intake, I limit my consumption of grain and pasta. Bread doesn't make the cut. A few years ago, I discovered a "keto" bread that felt and tasted like real bread. Suddenly, sandwiches are back on the list! Historically, *Dave's Killer Bread* is a go-to option for me when I have my mouth set on a fried egg sandwich. Ezekiel bread also makes the cut. *Dave's Killer Bread* is an all-natural, whole-grain hearty bread. But it's not keto. It's real bread. For several years, I ate keto bread. One day I was almost out of keto bread and my wife snagged a fresh loaf on the way home from work—some *Dave's Killer Bread*. I wanted to make two fried egg sandwiches, using the last two slices of keto bread and two slices of Dave's. I made a curious discovery. Keto bread doesn't toast. I can toast it for 10 minutes and it barely changes color. It gets hard and crumbly, but not toasty. Dave's bread toasts in a few short minutes, turns a golden brown, and remains richly chewy in the center. Keto bread seems like it's real bread, but it ain't. It doesn't behave like real bread in one of the primary functions of bread, which is to toast.

I don't know what they put in fake bread to make it seem real, but it defies the natural order of things. What it does inside my body is anyone's guess. I now rarely eat keto bread. I eat real bread or I don't eat any. I apply this same logic to other foods as well. Only by exception ought one to eat pretend ice cream (fat-free), fake butter (margarine), or egg whites only. That we eat eggs makes sense, but as the only mammals who consume milk from other species, I'm wary about dairy.

Candy is supposed to have sugar, beer alcohol, and coffee caffeine. Granted, there is a time and a place for a cup of decaf coffee. The first duty of wine is to be red. I have a hunch that fish skin, fruit seeds, and grease are good for you. I'm not a nutritionist, but a part of me is resistant to a replica of anything that bastardizes its natural state, whether for convenience or "health." Most of the time, it seems that nature encourages us to enjoy the real thing or to not have it at all. Martin Luther said, "Sin boldly." Be or don't be, but never pretend. Incidentally, this applies directly to social media profiles. Sermon concluded.

I read once that most marriages would improve dramatically if spouses treated each other with the same courtesy and respect that they do strangers in public. I'm kind to the barista, but when I get home, I take the gloves off. It's something like "we hurt the ones we love", but I find that the important lesson is consistency of character. Character is not something that I compartmentalize or that applies differently in different contexts. If I am a respectful person, I extend that respect in every area of my life. If I am respectful to my boss but not my spouse, I'm not a respectful person. Instead, I'm an expedient actor. How I do one thing is how I do everything. On a first date, if your date is a jerk to the server, he's a jerk, period. How I treat those closest to me *is how I am*. That barometer provides vital information as I assess myself and potential areas for improvement.

When you need to buy a tool and plan to keep it after the project is over, buy the best tool you can afford. Quality tools work better, are more enjoyable to use, and they last longer. I own tools that used to belong to my father and they still work. Crappy tools make things harder and add needless frustration. Inevitably, when they break, it is during a project when I need them most. The same principle applies to kitchen equipment, knives, guns, and boots. Incidentally, own a good bed and a good pair of shoes; if you're not in one, you're in the other. Don't settle for imitation versions of original things. In a world replete with cheap plastic and disposable everything, don't be a bargain knock-off or a cheap replica of the person you are designed to be. Mix simplicity with utility and add a dash of personal style. Own things that last and be a person who lasts.

Relax. As you commit you will be tempted to achieve everything all at once. You can't. Do one thing at a time and do it well.

An ancient Master lovingly and carefully crafted a sailboat. With his gleaming eyes and practiced hands he planed her curves, notched and sanded each board to create seamless lines, and sturdied her bow for high winds and rough seas. When he was satisfied, he lashed a full, bright sail to her mast to capture the wind. Once christened, she flew across the open sea, gathering the horizon, her sails aflame with sunlight and her spray glistening like diamonds. Sadly, she fell into the hands of a dark-hearted pirate. He bashed and neglected her as he raged on the ocean, feasting on blood and treasure. As the Fates would have it, she returned one day to the Master's harbor.

Her sail was torn, her deck sunbaked and chipping, and her bow sagged loosely. Once so beautiful and free, she was ashamed to meet the Master in her neglected condition. But the Master was delighted to have her home, thinking he had lost her forever. He pulled her to the safety of his boathouse and ran his hands along her lines, remembering. He said, "I can feel your heartbreak. I see how heavily you now rest on the water. Take heart. The sea is forever open, the horizon still calls, and the sun burns as it always has. We will restore what the storms have taken. The wind will carry you again across the deep blue promise and into everything that is." The Master began that very day. He worked from each sunrise and into the nights of stars until she was made whole again. She was new, reborn, but now seasoned and tested by salt and storm and challenge, a vessel worthy of her calling. The hard years we spend at sea prepare us for our calling.

In the world of precision shooting, there is an adage that "slow is smooth, and smooth is fast." Some add, "And fast is sexy." When you *try* to draw, aim, and shoot fast, the clamoring results in mistakes. Relax. Slow down, move like liquid, and the speed takes care of itself. Try less hard and do more better. Don't sweat the small stuff. Eliminate needless effort. Get slow and get smooth. Establish a rhythm. Become more of a sailboat than a rowboat.

Paraphrasing Stockdale, if you must be a prisoner, be a slow-moving, cagey one. Big Bob used to say, "If you don't have time to do it right, how do you have time to do it over?" Keep your wits about you, pay attention, and glide. Do what must be done, avoid what is unnecessary, and take the rest in stride. Engage the closest target and worry about the distant targets when you get to them. Allow tomorrow's problems to reside in the morrow. Today there are enough resident problems. Don't allow problems from tomorrow to immigrate and overcrowd today. Stride and glide.

Sticking to a chosen course of action requires commitment. Sustained commitment is fueled by enjoyment or purpose. Enjoyment and purpose are derived from immersion in an activity and the ambient sense of contributing to the common good. What I need to effectively commit is increased depth, not scope. Csikszentmihalyi writes of "The Autotelic Self." "The difference between someone who enjoys life and someone who is overwhelmed by it is a product of a combination of such external factors and the way a person has come to interpret them—that is, whether he sees challenges as threats or as opportunities for action . . . The autotelic self is one that easily translates potential threats into enjoyable challenges, and therefore maintains its inner harmony. A person who is never bored, seldom anxious, involved with what goes on, and in flow most of the time . . ."[48]

Csikszentmihalyi suggests that the rules for self-development along these lines are simple: 1) set goals and recognize corresponding challenges, which suggest the skills needed to address them; 2) Become immersed in the activity through concentration (investing attention); 3) Pay attention to what is happening, filtering out distractions and 4) Learn to enjoy the immediate experience.

"Being in control of the mind means that literally anything that happens can be a source of joy . . . To achieve this control . . . requires determination and discipline. Optimal experience is not the result of a hedonistic, lotus-eating approach to life. A relaxed, laissez-faire attitude is not a sufficient defense against chaos . . . one must develop skills that stretch capabilities, that make one become more

---

[48] *Flow*, 209.

than what one is. Flow drives individuals to creativity and outstanding achievement. The necessity to develop increasingly refined skills to sustain enjoyment is what lies behind the evolution of culture. It motivates both individuals and cultures to change into more complex entities. The rewards of creating order in experience provide the energy that propels evolution—they pave the way for those dimly imagined descendants of ours, more complex and wise than we are, who will soon take our place."[49]

---

[49] Ibid., 213.

5

Character (Being and Service)

A person's character is the sum of their characteristics, or who they are *known as*. I've often heard that character is who you are when no one is watching. Character is like health; we all have it whether good or bad. Characteristics, or personality traits, may or may not be virtuous. Everyone has *a* character. In common usage, however, a person *of character* is typically thought to be someone of high moral or ethical standing or who abides by principles. Character development is often used to describe one's development of a moral compass by which to guide decisions and actions. To say that something is *out of character* for a person indicates a deviation from their norm.

For this book, and as character relates to commitment, the "norm" defines the core characteristic baseline of an individual. You are *like that*. What you are like flows naturally from you and serves as a baseline to which anomalies naturally return. Becoming a boxer is a focus on becoming a person who naturally embodies the characteristics of the version of yourself you admire most. It is the result of long obedience toward conforming to a reality organized around love instead of fear, with attending economies, principles, laws, and physics. You are *that* without trying. It is the intentional shaping, through diligent assessment, strategic planning, and disciplined execution, of the core of who you are. Perseverance proves character. The core of who I am, when forged in the fires of discipline, honesty, and corrective action, becomes a harbor to which I can retreat at any time, my inner citadel, what Thomas Merton (more on Merton below) calls the "secret place." The trials and tribulations of life become opportunities to show less ass and more heart. For it is during challenges that character is revealed. I am not as much the man who *responds* after careful consideration as he who *reacts* when caught off guard and put on the spot.

In emotional moments, I can't fake it. Unpleasant surprises, aggravation, and moments of anger are useful barometers to determine the condition of my character, the deepest condition of my heart. As I set goals and strive to achieve them, the strength of my character is revealed by my ability to keep promises, especially those I make to myself. When a simple "yes" or "no" means exactly that when I say it, no more and no less, requiring no justification or explanation, I know that I am on my way. Instead of anger, when the result of things not going my way is interested observation and calm acceptance, the walls of my inner citadel have been stacked high. From that place I can be a more useful human being.

They Can Kill You but They Can't Eat You. In moments when I recognize the sheer futility of externally directed efforts to control the world around me, I laugh. It feels equivalent to bailing water out of the sinking Titanic using a thimble. Incremental improvement in the cessation of pointless or aimless activity pays off exponentially in a generalized sense of *lightness*. The density of futility, ignited by a maelstrom of emotional turbulence around it, carries a weight disproportionate to its size or the place in my life that it occupies. Even the effort to control the behavior of one other person can be consuming.

The systemic tax is high and the payoff is either zero or of negative value. Curtailing efforts to control that which I simply cannot control produces a dramatic change in my overall disposition. As energy is saved or redirected, my mental landscape opens. As it turns out, there is a lot of space in my mind when it's not cluttered with open loops, unmet needs, irrational desires, competing beliefs, and a running kangaroo court where the world stands as defendant and I sit as Judge. On one hand, organizing my life using a system like <u>Getting Things Done</u> is invaluable to decluttering my mind. On the other hand, I must organize internally generated thoughts, wants, and feelings toward the end of generating fewer of those things, but of higher relevance and quality.

The most surprising effect that I experienced as my mind became less populated was amusement. I found it increasingly easy to enjoy what I was doing and to delight in details that I was unused to noticing. I watched a movie once that started in black-and-white. As the protagonist had a slow awakening of some mystical sort, he began to see in color. It came slowly at first but by the end of the movie, he saw everything in color. His power to see in color was related to the development of a sixth sense and psychic abilities. My ability to see in color depends upon acceptance of "what happens", a willingness to immerse myself fully in living through and with activity, shutting down the misery factory, and firing the entire union that runs it (i.e., the voices in my head). When it's closing time, you can go anywhere you like but you can't stay here.

A biblical proverb says that "a merry heart does good like a medicine." A historical saint said something like, "We are created to worship God and *enjoy him forever.*" Ben Franklin pointed to beer as proof that "God loves us and wants us to be happy." Mark Twain said, "Happiness is when what you think, what you say, and what you do are in harmony. I am determined to be cheerful and happy in whatever situation I may find myself. For I have learned that the greater part of our misery or unhappiness is determined not by our circumstances but by our disposition." Twain also said, "To get the full value of joy you must have someone to divide it with." What happens matters less than how I *perceive* what happens and human connection is essential. It may also come as a relief that we are not *required* to be happy.

Happiness is not a "right" that I "deserve." Why would I believe that a self-centered, mismanaged, or malevolent soul deserved happiness? It seems likely to me that opportunities to be happy are earned by becoming the type of person for whom happiness makes sense. Intentionally create a life where happiness is a welcome, expected, and frequent visitor.

The greatest weapons a soldier has in war to maintain sanity and footing are dark humor and tribal connection.

Soldiers in war joke and laugh about topics that are insensitive, impolite, and even twisted or macabre, what I've heard referred to as "gallows humor." On Camp Fallujah, 2004, an incoming rocket struck a portable latrine and killed the Marine seated inside it. The camp was infuriated. Back home, a traveling music festival called Lollapalooza was popular.

On the wall of one of the remaining latrines a Marine scrawled "The LollaFallujah Tour – where the nightlife is explosive!" Recalling this, I am at once shocked and saddened by the seeming irreverence. When I read it there, in *that place*, I got it. It was morbidly funny. We all knew it could have been any one of us and that there was nothing any of us could do about it. Laughter displaces fear. On that same deployment, during an operational lull, my buddy and I decided to throw on our vests and jog the inner perimeter of the camp.

We had not completed a full lap when a rocket detonated in an open field about 100 meters from us. We heard the ripping sound in the air as it flew over. We froze in our tracks. Surviving what felt like a close call elicited from my buddy the deadpan comment, "I hate running anyway." We both exploded in laughter and walked back to our hooch. That was the last time I voluntarily ran on that deployment. Marines and soldiers laugh because laughter is healing. The alternative to laughter is fear, bitterness, and contempt. The ability to laugh in the face of death ensures a higher-than-average chance of surviving death. It also guards against residual toxicity long after the war is over.

The road to character can feel heavy with prescriptions, programs, steps, and discipline. There's always *something*. The work never ends. We're never finished. The only way I know to find joy in a life that requires incessant doing is to learn to en-joy – *to fill with joy* – what I'm doing. I must learn to love what is necessary to do. Also, I must cultivate joy in the word "No."

My time on this earth is my time in the wilderness. In this wilderness, there are many valleys. I will walk through the valley of the Shadow of Death. Sometimes, I am afraid. Times of change are often this. I cannot escape this valley. Thomas Merton, writer, monk, and international ambassador for peace, wrote extensively and captured in unique artwork his traffic with darkness and silence. For Merton, the figurative darkness became not a place of malevolence or visionless chaos, but an inverted testament to his human inability to understand God's light. His 27 years in the monastery of Gethsemani in Kentucky were a silent vigil he kept, waiting for a divine light he knew he would never know in this life. Still, he remained. He wrote, "Your brightness is my darkness.

I know nothing of You and, by myself, I cannot even imagine how to go about knowing You. If I imagine You, I am mistaken. If I understand you, I am deluded. If I am conscious and certain I know You, I am crazy. The darkness is enough." Merton recognized that though he could not understand it, returning again and again to the Void awakened his soul to that which cannot be known, cannot be described, and cannot be captured. He experienced that the Void was not empty but teeming with Divine presence and power. He became a true earthly sojourner, he who would pass over this life as a bridge but never settle on it, longing to "return to the Father, to the Immense, to the Primordial, to the Unknown, to Him Who loves, to the Silent, to the Holy, to the Merciful, to Him Who is All." (Montaldo, xiii-xv)

Not long ago, I experienced a 10-day period that disrupted my existential sense of place and my concept of who I *am*. I entered and (barely) completed a 7-mile obstacle race. The day prior during the half-day drive to the venue was like any other. I was excited about the experience, enjoyed the drive with my good friend, and, after we ate a delicious dinner, I slept well. Twenty minutes into the race, my body ached in pain and I felt as if the electrical power had been cut off from my brain and my physical fuel tank had been emptied. I've had enough experience with endurance events to know that I was not ill-prepared, physically or nutritionally. As my condition worsened, I struggled to walk between the obstacles and felt as if I was approaching the end of my life as I knew it.

The unraveling was deep and internal psychological structures crumbled, or so it seemed. Something was not right. My will was barely strong enough to take each next step and soon I began walking around obstacles, knowing that I could not negotiate them. It got weird. Having run this race prior and having completed an intense hour-long fitness event only two weeks prior, I somehow knew that my current physical condition was a result of something profound at the existential energy level of my psyche, something spiritual. I have neither the education nor a history with experiences like this to have understood it then or to adequately explain it now. A week later, having endured days of mental cloudiness, emotional exhaustion, and physical pain, I was too depleted to do anything but lie motionless on my sofa.

As I sat down, I was struck by a notion that what I was experiencing was a kind of "soul sickness", an idea with which I am only vaguely familiar, but it captures the only apt description. I believe that this kind of "sickness" is one part of significant psycho-spiritual transitions when that which has successfully sustained you for so long is depleted and the reservoir from which you have drank is empty. It is vital to recognize that efforts to refill this reservoir are futile. I must find a new spring.

After unsuccessfully attempting a nap, I began to listen only to the sound of my breathing. What came to my mind was a thought so crisp and clear that I could not deny its instruction, "Turn your face to the sun." It carried a literal weight and a weight of literalness. I drove to a nearby park and slowly shuffled to a bench on the far side facing the sun. I sat, spread my arms, and let the sunlight warm my face. As my body began to warm in the December air, I removed my sweater and then my shirt. I sat, stripped to the waist, and the sun soaked into my skin for over half an hour. As it did, images began to appear in my mind, snapshots of humans across time.

There were sailors on wooden ships, a baby born in a farm field, laborers building the pyramids of Egypt, and a Spartan soldier standing in the quiet calm after battle. In a moment I knew that each of them and billions more had felt what I was feeling in the moment. I was part of the interminable line of humans who rely upon and take pleasure in our constant companion, that mysterious star that warms our days, fills our world with light, grows our food, and sets with the moon the day-night rhythm of life on Earth. In the nourishment of its warmth and the momentary connection to all living things, I was reborn. *Reborn* seems an exaggerated or worn-out word, but it is the only approximation I can devise to describe the effect.

When I rose from the bench, I was restored. Physically and emotionally, I was relieved of pain. I was drawing energy from a new tank (of feeling and connection) and my network was alive with electricity. I walked across the lawn to my car as though I had just woken up from a long and confusing dream. The shift endures and each day seems to have about it a newness and an expectation that was long missing from my vision. Maybe Mama Kay was right all those years ago, when she said, "If you can't tone it, tan it!"

As a young Marine, I hung on the wall of my office an Adlai Stevenson quote, a gift to me from a true gunfighter. "On the plains of hesitation lie the blackened bones of countless millions who, at the dawn of victory, sat down to rest, and in resting died." Should I rest in the valley, my fate is that of shrouding darkness and death. What I can muster, with the Allfather's help, is a single step. I will take it. Lord willing, I will take another after it. Taken in sequence, I will now forever know that one day I will make it to the bright clearing in the wilderness and once again turn my face to the sun.

As I age, there are fewer dragons to slay and more gardens that need planting. I was ceaselessly restless as a young man, as many of us are. Having ventured out of Eden into the badlands of the world (a developmental necessity), I desire nothing more now than a final homecoming.

Homecoming is *reintegration*. The reintegration of a person's shadow is a homecoming. As I mature through my teen and young adult years, I draw from the cultural expectations in which I live to cobble together a version of self that I feel will be widely accepted. Informed by my culture, I decide what is good and bad, to build a rickety version of "me" from the acceptable wood and toss the unacceptable wood into the shadow. Unfortunately, culture itself is a *relative* measure of good and bad, for apparent cultural differences across the world take drastically different views on the same thing. Johnson uses *individuality* and *selflessness* as examples.

Individuality is prized in the West and deplored in the East. We witness on the global geopolitical scene the destructive clash of these two ideals. I construct a straw man who is supposed to be me, which I unremittingly present to my world, while key elements of my person languish in my shadow, slowly gaining energy. The most heartbreaking sacrifice I make is the relegation of the very best of who I might be to my shadow. My cultural filter is too fine to allow what Johnson calls the gold in the shadow to shine. Jordan Peterson talks about dragons. Mythologically, heroes must fight dragons. Why? Because dragons have gold. They are the dormant terrors waiting to burn our cities to ashes. They must be vanquished, lest their constant threat erode our peace.

By slaying them, I at once settle the threat and gain access to the hoarded gold. When I am willing to face the horror of the dragon, trekking to its lair in my shadow, armed with the sword and shield of truth, mustering courage step by step, I find the most terrifying of beasts. Yet, wielding truth, I discover that the beast bleeds when cut. I find that it is not *all the dragons in the world*, it is a *single* dragon. By facing it, in the heat of it, I forget that it once ruled my entire kingdom with its lore. By plunging my truth into it again and again, it weakens. Truth protects me from its fire. Its threat is real, but my fear of it is a fiction that I've written, monstrous and all-encompassing. When it finally falls, my kingdom – *the range of my effective will* (Willard) – is free of it. I am free to carry its gold, the best parts of my potential that it has hidden from me and guarded, into my life to spend how I wish.

Recently, I found a scrap of paper in an old book in my personal library. It was a note to self from 15 years ago. I used to write like this to myself, get fired up, and then turn on the afterburners until the fuel ran out. It was like finding a time capsule. *"Return to the code. Remember the beacon.*

Remember The Call. Keep your honor clean. Be above reproach. Do justly. Love mercy. Walk humbly. Show respect. Listen. Each day, speak fewer words than the last and you will approach wisdom. Redeem the time. Be accountable. Be dependable. It doesn't matter what you say, it matters what you do. It doesn't matter just what you do, it matters how you do it. You can change. A new day is possible. See how the morning sun warms the Earth? Life can warm you in the same way. Now is now. Accept now. Don't wrestle with forever. Remember your promises. Keep them. Recognize your dragon and slay it." Now, I must take the long view. In the park where I sit, there are no longer dragons. There is only sunlight in which I must learn to silently sit.

After all that has happened, I feel a whole lot more like I do now than I did when I got here. Regardless of what we do or do not do, we change over time. Willard said that character formation occurs in two ways, intentionally or unintentionally, but that it always occurs. I am free to decide the type of person I admire and become more like that. I am also free to let life shape me until the increasing velocity of entropy destroys the ship and I end in ruin, "a pair of ragged claws scuttling across the floors of silent seas", as T.S. Eliot described. Ungoverned, the state of my being, my soul, devolves into chaos. Experiencing chaos in the skies of oblivion can be temporarily fun, but it ends with a hard landing.

The joke is on me. I search for "God" to discover that "God" is not hidden. If the Kingdom of the Heavens truly is all around me, "at hand", I need only recognize it in the mundane to experience and enjoy it. A "spiritual awakening" occurs when I recognize and am conscious of a dynamic life force imbued in everything, what Peterson called a "Benevolent Force for Good" that operates autonomously in my life. My charge is not to create power in my life, but simply to tap into it. I am not required to "do" much, but to do my part to simply accept and exist within the laws and powers of nature as beneficiary or victim, as I choose.

Character and power go together. The record of my past life is not the basis upon which my future life will be judged. Oscar Wilde said, "Never judge anyone shortly because every saint has a past and every sinner has a future." J.D. Crow once told me that what comes most often before a spiritual awakening is a rude awakening. We have a blank page before us. We are invited to write our own story and to punch our ticket into a life of sanity, purpose, utility, and peace of mind. When the doors are flung open, what rushes in with the sunlight is the belly laugh of Father Time, encouraging us to make the most of it.

I Cut it Three Times and It's Still too Short. Big Bob said that. He was a woodworker and craftsman. He'd follow it up by telling me to get the "board stretcher" out of the truck. The image of a man scratching his head while trying to figure out why repeatedly cutting a board doesn't lengthen it remains funny to me. It's funny because it reminds me of how blind I can be to my patterns of behavior as the cause for the results I repeatedly get.

When you realize that you've been doing the same thing for years and expecting different results, laughter strikes me as the best choice from the available options. We're all idiots in this way. It's essential to take your work seriously, but it is perilous to take yourself seriously. Amplified self-seriousness lies at the heart of many dysfunctions, oversensitivity, anxiety, disappointment, calcification, histrionics, bitterness, and the delusion that I inhabit the center of the universe.

It begins with the deception that "getting what I want" will make me happy. My ego thinks that it's me and regards itself and its survival as of utmost importance. Very serious. This breeds an oversensitivity to perceived slights of any kind and disproportionate emotional retaliation. My ego is perpetually overstimulated and feels threatened, choosing from any one of four primal options: fight, flight, posture, or submit. After decades of back-break and heart-break to accumulate things and win fights that amount to very little I care about, I feel like a punchline to a joke. I'd gladly trade my G-wagon for one chance to "play that game again", "show up to that wedding", "talk to my grandfather one more time", or to "tell her I'm sorry." I have invested heavily and found the returns unsatisfying. It feels like a bait-and-switch. I thought I did everything "right."

In truth, I got exactly what I asked for. I plotted my course according to the map and information that I'd been given, including the "rules" for play, and I played two-dimensional life chess to the best of my ability. After winning and losing countless games, committing costly mistakes, stacking a few trophies and medals, and making friends with fellow competitors, I have a life.

One day, I show up for a chess match (or deal negotiation, job interview, promotion) and I don't care whether I win. I want to care but I don't. I try to make myself care with a fiery pep talk and a little shadow boxing, but when I sit down to compete, I simply want to play. The choreography of the moves as strategy meets strategy assumes a connectedness and beauty it once lacked. I notice for the first time that the pieces themselves are hand-carved and burnished, each with its own story, carrying a nick from being dropped or the dark shadow of oil from a thousand thumbs.

I am more interested in my opponent and her story than in the combat of our game. My interest is diverted from cognitive strategy and tactical expression on the board to wishing to know more about her as a person, not as a competitor. When did she start playing? Who is her favorite chess master? Why does she love the game? The contest is no longer the reason I am here, but merely the vehicle through which like-minded people can congregate and connect.

I realize that it's *a game* and the rules of the game feel contrived. I feel no urgency between moves and no impatience while waiting for my opponent to make a move. I don't care if I win. I don't mind whether we finish the game. We're two people sitting together moving tiny statues around on a checkerboard based on a tacit agreement that *this is how things are*. Life feels suspiciously like theater. Where's the improv? These feelings are foreign. I don't understand them.

What I have discovered and felt are the energies of my inferior function displacing the energy of my superior function. When I have fully explored and expressed the reaches of my superior thinking function, the life-giving energy it has always yielded on my behalf subsides. Always reliable, it becomes unreliable. As the energies of another function rise in its place, it is as though new dimensions appear in the same activity. Playing life chess becomes a 3-dimensional game. Untapped functions within our shadows have the power to give us vision. My granny used to say, "Wellness is a crown a healthy man wears that only the sick can see." I do not need a new life, but the vision to see the one I have in a new way. I then pass through the narrow gate to the heavens.

Let the Fates Decide. There was a time in the not-too-distant past when humans believed that human life was divinely scripted. The Greeks and Vikings called it Fate, from which a man's destiny manifested. Practically, one could not deny Fate, for a person's choices would inevitably lead him or her toward their fated end. In partial jest, I often flip a coin to make decisions, offering, "Let the Fates decide" as I flip it. Unless it concerns an area where I have significant experience combined with deep knowledge, flipping a coin is as likely to provide a good choice as making it myself.

Every decision feels important but, in the context of my life's trajectory, few are. The Chinese *I Ching*, translated

Book of Changes, is at once philosophical, cosmological, and a divination manual. Like Kabbalah priests who could predict the future through numerical analysis of the Torah, the *I Ching* prescribes a method for cleromancy, where randomly generated numbers arranged in six rows form a hexagram that reveals the wishes or "prediction" of a deity concerning probable outcomes. Confucianism, Taoism, and Buddhism all have integrated elements of the I Ching. The I Ching version of casting lots is the equivalent of rolling a 64-sided dice (or die, if you're old-fashioned). As I stare into the web-like complexity of my system of systems and across the world stage, it is like a finely woven spider's web where every thread is a path and every intersection a decision.

In trying to reach the center, an almost limitless combination of decisions will lead me there. Assuming I take very few paths backward and frequent paths forward, I can take a left or right turn at any time and will eventually reach the center. The burden of making the "correct" decision at any juncture is relieved by the knowledge that even semi-controlled randomness would not prevent me from making progress. I am free to call it like I see it in a specific moment, to flip a coin, or to roll a 64-sided dice. All decisions are a dice roll regardless. We cannot think through every possibility. But there are no mistakes or missteps, for each path is sufficient unto itself for the lessons it will offer. Life repeatedly offers me the chance to learn a lesson until I finally learn it. It is not a straight line from the gutter to the right hand of God. All worthwhile roads lead to the Center. Roll the dice.

In the world of "superforecasting" (*The Good Judgement Project*), individuals and think tanks attempt to predict things like major financial or geopolitical events. Superforecasters are defined by being statistically correct more often than the average expert. Accounting for historical trends and using mathematical models, forecasters make comparisons, include average opinions, and adjust for predictable biases. Studies indicate that superforecasters aren't better readers of information than their non-super counterparts but are better at *filtering noise*. They detect the most probable outcome by eliminating what is least probable or irrelevant. Like Michelangelo, they simply chip away everything that is not the sculpture.

As energy wanes in my superior function, it thrusts me into a hinge or transition period. My reaction is to determine what next to do. Once attempts to recruit additional fuel for my superior function fail, I realize that I've encountered an existential question. It is not what to *do* but how to *be*. My relationship with the world has changed. I am used to *being* a certain way based on action, i.e., *acting* a certain way, but seeing the world through my superior function has lost its vitality. Repeated attempts to reignite that function are met with failure or, worse, become an unsuitable farcical pantomime, reference the old bald guy in slip-on Vans and a Metallica t-shirt driving the convertible Corvette (I have both a pair of Vans and an old Metallica t-shirt, but I can't afford a Corvette, so I judge).

Fifty-year-old men acting like they're twenty-one has a specific, intrinsic, and recognizable sadness to it because it showcases human need colliding with ignorant futility. I don't fit *there* anymore. I'm *here* now and I can't go back. *I don't know what to do.* This is a pivotal opportunity to embrace and channel the energy of inferior functions and see the world through a new lens, instead of attempting to reclaim youth. Scripture says that unless a person becomes like a little child, they cannot see the heavens. This does not encourage immaturity, or not acting your age, but openness to seeing the world anew. Tackling life through an inferior function feels much like a child learning a new skill. It's like learning to write with your non-dominant hand. The experience is profound. In my case, switching from relating to the world through my thinking function (ideas and abstractions) to exploring it through sensation (tangible objects and people) was to discover hidden dimensions that were there all along. In this sense, I don't *create* a new reality, I *discover* one.

The formation of character over time requires a periodic refitting of myself into the context of my life. As I change, so does my life or how I perceive it. My perception is what makes it so. As I fertilize and tend to the trees I want to bear fruit, I must also prune and discard dying branches. Some trees must be uprooted altogether. There will be death. There will also be growth and regrowth. New life takes the form of new branches growing from an old trunk.

Cultural Theater. To enjoy a movie charged with unimaginable creatures, inhuman feats of strength, and computer-generated imagery requires the "suspension of disbelief." Suspension of disbelief is a tacit agreement that viewers make with producers not to second guess the "reality" presented in the film. I watch movies not because they are factual, but because afford me a chance to live vicariously in another reality. I seek entertainment and am willing to forego realism to enjoy it. Societies function in much the same way. Our government tells us a story and we all agree to behave as though it's true. It's what Noam Chomsky called the "Manufacture of Consent", where both sides of the argument are scripted and the masses can "choose" a side. What the masses are discouraged from doing is creating a third option that contends with the others. In socialist governments, the rule of law is exerted externally.

Behavior is controlled through fear and punishment is meted out liberally. The government owns everything and the citizenry is paid subsistence wages. A lack of ownership is supposed to eliminate class struggles. It does not, but merely widens the gap between affluence and subsistence. In democratic countries, the rule of law is exerted internally via a national myth to which we all agree.

Behavior is controlled through beliefs. Individuals are allowed to own property and businesses, a requisite to living the American Dream. In truth, we've been tricked into thinking that we "own" things through mortgages and financing options. I don't own my home, the bank does. Even when I am diligent enough to pay off my mortgage, the insurance and tax burdens persist. The government will always get their cut. The U.S. economy requires perpetual consumption for the economic machine to continue running. From permits to raw materials to manufacturing and supply chains, imports and exports, to the checkout stand to registrations and balance sheets, up to and including one's post-mortem estate, the government taxes at every turn, from cradle to beyond the grave.

American citizens labor under a false assumption that they are building something for themselves, or their heirs, but free and clear ownership is not a reality, even in capitalistic societies. Nonetheless, capitalism (and the legal protection of land rights) has done more for the global standard of living, medicine, creativity, and technology than any other system. The incentive to climb the socioeconomic ladder is illusory but powerful. Believing that I can rise from rags to riches through individual effort is enough to ignite the hottest fire of ambition, the real math of my effective tax rate notwithstanding. As a result, we have it better than most, but must bring cultural awareness to our plight of integration.

One result of a culture based on conspicuous consumption is the fallacy that I must own one each of everything. Homeownership is touted as a "right" for every American. Each person must own a vehicle, or at least finance one and pretend to own it. If I have a yard, I must own a lawn mower and an array of landscaping tools. I also must own appropriate footwear for every occasion, sixteen cozy blankets scattered throughout my house, four versions of the same jacket, and every kitchen gadget invented, just in case I ever cook that special dish. On my street, two of my neighbors have lawns the size of the endzone on a football field. They *each* own a riding lawn mower.

My closets and dressers are stuffed with more clothes than I could wear out in a lifetime, categorized by activity. I have distinct outfits for work, church, gym, weekends, swimming pools, nights out, weddings/funerals, camping, yard work, and job interviews. Within each, I might have subcategories of "fat" clothes and "skinny" clothes, plus a special category of clothing received as gifts that I know I will never wear but cannot bring myself to discard. It's shocking to realize that when I was a kid I had only one pair of shoes, which I wore everywhere I went.

I distinctly recall having one pair of trousers and one pair of jeans, plus a single button-up shirt and a few T-shirts. In many countries I have visited, the "right" and requirement to own things is less pervasive. People borrow and share before they buy. When an individual does not have enough, the collective compensates. As a community, we have enough. Each family does not have to be a self-sufficient island unto themselves. The wealth of the U.S. has provided our country with unparalleled services, roads, museums, monuments, libraries, and local, state, and national parks that are preserved and open to the public. Learning to enjoy things without owning them and learning to share what we have is a step away from egoic illusions and toward grounded being.

Seneca said, "We own only that which cannot be lost in shipwreck." The road to character formation is marked not by accrual and consumption, but by the shattering of external illusion and conscious investment in those internal qualities that endure. Character is more important than accomplishment. These are the "treasures in heaven" mentioned in the Bible, where moth and rust do not corrupt, and those of enduring value kept in the heart. Accordingly, the formation of timeless virtues will shape and curtail my desires. My inventory of shiny objects becomes less relevant. It's not that I don't appreciate a fine automobile or an heirloom-quality wristwatch, but my values shift. Those things become less interesting.

I begin to place a higher value on how I experience the world than what I can get from it. Mark Twain said, "The perfection of wisdom, and the end of true philosophy is to proportion our wants to our possessions, our ambitions to our capacities, we will then be a happy and virtuous people." I must cultivate a desire for things of absolute value and occupy a place of healthy indifference to that which can be lost at sea or stolen from my parked car.

Memento Mori and Memento Vivere. "Remember you must die" and "Remember you must live." When I discover that I have cancer and six months to live, my priorities are jolted. I must contend with my mortality and the inevitability of death. Soldiers, police officers, and adrenaline junkies stare into the abyss. Sometimes, the abyss stares back. We all have a chronic disease. Nobody gets out alive. Death will come when it comes. Even the cancer patient and the doctors don't "know" when death will come. Nor do we. But we know that it will. If I keep it in the back of my mind and intentionally contemplate it regularly, I may be better able to live accordingly. I can live in concert with the priorities of the dying.

Contending with an inevitable death sentence can lead to nihilism, a view that life is a meaningless absurdity. Pessimism and skepticism accompany. Conversely, existentialism emphasizes the agency of the individual, who is free and responsible for their development and the quality of their life, and it wrestles with how to derive meaning from perceived absurdity.

In either case, neither God nor the Fates play a role in human life, except as "an opiate for the masses", as Karl Marx said. Rationalists argue that some categories of truth can be directly grasped through intellect, based on an assumption that reality has an inherently logical structure, that math is the language of God, and that experience fails to produce certainty.

Rationalism fails at the margins. When experience cannot conform to reason – I can't believe my eyes! – the framework must be examined. If I cannot understand an experience, I believe it is more likely that my framework is inadequate than that the experience itself is untrue. In phenomenology, the lived experience of human beings is the primary source of meaning and from it, humans learn what is natural and unnatural or true and untrue through observation, perception, and the consideration of intentionality as the structure of experience. Scientific theories or philosophical abstractions are simply that, abstractions.

Living a life is a tangible experience and a sensory one. It's *real*. The gap between abstractions and my-life-in-this-moment is the problem. The conversion of ideas into kinetic material to reform the nature of my interactions with people and things feels as slippery as mercury and as mystical as alchemy. The experience of a single human is unreliable as a reference for truth but, in the context of "human experience" as a historical cannon compiled over thousands of years, individual experience underscores the lessons of scripture and philosophy.

History provides guideposts by which to navigate. My experience proves or disproves them. I can use the evidence to reshape my belief system. I grow from knowing *about* things to *knowing* them through experience, deep down in my *knower*. My mother once warned me to guard my heart, saying, "You don't fall in love when you learn another person's secrets; you fall in love when you tell them yours." In the same way, I don't "fall in love" with my life when I understand everything about it, but when I allow it to teach me about myself, one lesson at a time, and reveal the secrets I've kept from myself.

There is freedom in this. I am relieved of an impossible burden, for I will never understand everything. I will see in part, I will know in part, and I will wonder at the rest. In the meantime, if I truly believe that we are made for each other then I will begin to treat each person I meet as though they are the most important person in the world because, in the moment that I meet them, they are. If I truly believe any of a handful of maxims, I'll start to act like it.

Marcus Aurelius said, "You could leave life right now. Let that determine what you do and say and think." What I do, say, and think determines how I will be remembered—who I was *known as*. After I'm gone, the world's memory is short. By dying I simply make room for another. The best I can do is to prepare, so that when death arrives my affairs are in order, my regrets are few, and my work is done. In keeping with the pair of questions, "For what would you die" and "For what will you live", the flip side of *memento mori* is *memento vivere*, "Remember that you must live." In the Gnostic gospels, Jesus is quoted as saying, "Life is a bridge; pass over it but do not settle on it." To live a life of reasonable contentment and peace, I must travel light and free, unencumbered by the "cares of this world" which, like ankle weights, will pull me to the bottom of an ocean of inconsequential trifles.

The things I concern myself with must be few and foundational. I must return to them often and allow them to influence what I think, say, and do. When I envision the road to character as a bridge over troubled waters, I realize that the pain of walking such a path is a small price to pay to avoid a swim to the horizon, treading water on rough seas, or the feeling of sinking slowly into the darkness of the abyss. At least from the bridge, I have air and sunlight and fellow travelers to share it with. Marcus Aurelius said, "Love the discipline you know, and let it support you. Entrust everything willingly to the gods, and then make your way through life—no one's master and no one's slave."

Transformation. Robert A. Johnson, in *Transformation*, explains the evolution of masculine consciousness. He employs Don Quixote, Hamlet, and Faust to depict the primary characteristics of each phase, from "simple" to "complex" to "enlightened", as mentioned earlier. Respectively, these phases are 2-dimensional, 3-dimensional, and 4-dimensional. As character relates to being, a deeper understanding of these phases is useful for conceptualizing the journey from *here* to *there*.

In Don Quixote, he and his sidekick Sancho Panza illuminate the primary characteristics of the "simple" or 2-dimensional man. The Simple Man is a "red-blooded" human being propelled by instinct and fantasy. He has a direct, uncomplicated view of life. He sometimes lives in a vivid inner world at the expense of outer fact and reality. Mythologically, the Simple Man inhabits the Garden of Eden. Johnson uses the two characters to explain two facets of simple existence. Quixote wants to change the world but has no idea what the world is like. Sancho knows the world but has no desire to change it.

Johnson presents them as "pure spirit" and "pure flesh." "Don Quixote, with his roots deep in instinct and faith, is the man of courage who redeems anything that befalls him."[50] The delusional foibles of the pair as they set out to set right the wrongs of the world on a campaign of knighthood, romance, and chivalry. The tale is at once uncomfortably disastrous and terrifically humorous. Tragically, Quixote spends his last few hours dying as a 3-dimensional man. Realizing that his adventures were

---

[50] R. Johnson, *Transformation: Understanding the Three Levels of Masculine Consciousness* (New York: Harper One, 1991), 35.

fantasy, "unreal exercises of his imagination", he laments. Sancho switches roles with Quixote and admonishes him to continue the quest, but Quixote dies. "The true miracle of the story is the "sanchification" of Quixote and the "quixotification" of Sancho. The true journey of knighthood and chivalry has been to draw ego and shadow together, to diminish the split in personality indicated by the difference between the two. . ."[51] Johnson then turns to Hamlet to represent the 3-dimensional man.

"In Hamlet we find the man of tragedy, he who makes chaos and failure of everything he touches . . . Hamlet is the most profound example in all of literature of the divided man." (Ibid, 35) Hamlet fails to synthesize paradox within himself, that of masculine/feminine, order/chaos, or self/shadow. He is indecisive and "pale-blooded." Vacillation is his undoing, a hallmark of the Complex Man. Hamlet teaches us that the price of indecision is much higher than a "wrong" decision. He knows too much to be simple but not enough to be whole. He is caught between vision and practicality, that familiar gap between the abstract and the tangible. Hamlet can imagine a better world but lacks the means to realize it. Caught up in words, he cannot act. Also, he patently rejects, even destroys, the feminine beauty and wisdom available, as represented by Ophelia and his mother. "All feminine elements whither in the face of three-dimensional consciousness."[52]

---

[51] Ibid., 29.
[52] Ibid., 43.

He has been driven from Eden and knows he cannot return, but cannot grow beyond, or find redemption, so he languishes between nostalgia (the past) and anxiety (the future). Hamlet fails to bring to fruition either vision or practicality. He is strong enough to see but too weak to accomplish. "He is the prototype of so many modern men who see a noble world [or a noble vision of themselves] in their imaginations but don't have the means to accomplish it."[53]

Faust provides a model for a Complex Man who transitions to enlightenment through the integration of his shadow. The hinge period, as I describe it, between 3D and 4D consciousness is the "Dark Night of the Soul" captured in a Saint John of the Cross poem and subsequent treatise. Johnson elaborates, "This is the midlife crisis, the mute suffering of existential man . . . This is the experience of the intelligent man, the heroic man, the one who has reached the goal of modern consciousness . . . what happens when you reach the top of the ladder only to find that it was set up against the wrong wall. It is the very best man who suffers this Hamlet crisis."[54]

Johnson describes the Enlightened Man as a redeemed man, "gold-blooded", and whole. Referenced in a previous chapter, Johnson defines *happiness* as being in the happenings as they happen, or a version of that, and offers that being in what happens offers a bridge between the inner world and the objective fact of reality. The transition

---

[53] Ibid., 47.
[54] Ibid., 55.

from 3-D to 4-D requires a psychological break that reveals discipline and self-consciousness to be insufficient to usher a man to enlightenment. They got me *here* but they won't get me *there*. The break happens "just before the first redemptive vision of four-dimensional consciousness breaks through."[55] From the clash of creativity and destruction, enlightenment erupts. The presence of both is required for wholeness. Johnson explains that the "Heavenly Jerusalem" represents an enlightened Garden of Eden.

At a mythological level, man's search for the Holy Grail and myths like it equate to a search for enlightenment. Ironically, venturing "out there" to search for the Grail takes us further from it, as it is located *at hand*, but the experience of the quest is necessary. I must consume the energy of my divided self before I can seek with vision the integration that is my homecoming and, ideally, the discovery of the grail where I started. This integration is Jung's integration of the shadow with my ego, which Johnson explains through the archetypal fusion of Ego (Faust) and Shadow (Mephistopheles).[56] *"Encountering the shadow means rediscovering the unlived faculties of one's life, not following any prescribed formula for change."*[57]

Experiencing the unlived portions of one's life without attachment is a prescription for freedom. For that to occur requires the introduction of a fourth force to the Holy

---

[55] Ibid., 57.
[56] Ibid., 53.
[57] Ibid., 61.

Trinity, the Devil. The Devil is essential to religion. Without evil in that context, there's not much to discuss. Mythologically, this combination is order and chaos. Psychologically, in the consciousness of man, it is the synthesis of the known and unknown, or the fully developed and the ignored—my ego and my shadow. Johnson is careful to point out that the "unlived life" is not to be taken literally. Lost youth cannot be recovered by dressing and acting like a teenager. Those years are behind us. We can't go back. He warns, "Few misconceptions of modern man cost him so heavily as this tendency toward literalness."[58]

Instead, Johnson encourages exploration into imagination, symbol, art, ritual, and creation as media to experience and integrate inferior functions. The ego remains necessary to govern the process and maintain stability. But the ego as head honcho must be replaced, that is, recentered in the Great Spirit, the unifying and benevolent force that saturates the universe and of which the known universe is merely a small part. Johnson describes this as a painful "dethroning" of the ego. It is akin to death and captured in the paradox of losing one's life to find it. The ego must be put in its proper place, subservient to the Greater Good. "It is the unity of life, not the triumph of one faculty over another, that is the goal of imagination, fantasy, and ceremony."[59]

---

[58] Ibid., 67.
[59] Ibid., 71.

In the end, Faust falls victim to breaking a fatal rule, but is redeemed nonetheless and Mephistopheles with him. Like Quixote and Sancho, Faust and Mephistopheles are redeemed by becoming like each other and by love, for "at the gates of heaven, it is grace, not justice, that prevails."[60]

Summum Bonum. The highest good for which we were collectively made and the bedrock upon which a framework of ethical actions, when consistently pursued, results in the best possible life.

Stoic philosophy highlights three relationships:

   a.   With the body you inhabit;
   b.   With the divine, the cause of all things;
   c.   With the people around you.[61]

Humans are meant to connect. We cannot deny our nature, but must do that for which we were designed, like any invention, tool, piece of furniture, animal, or fruit tree. Utility and service for the common good are those expressions for which we were perfectly designed. The strategy is to relocate – i.e., surrender – my center of gravity to a power greater than myself, that of the greater good. The contrived life I lose in this scenario is of little value in light of the life I find.

I wrote previously that I discovered the word "*sonder*" a few years ago, a fleeting moment when I am aware that everyone around me—the passerby, the clerk at the counter, the woman sitting alone in the corner—has a life

---

[60] Ibid., 95.
[61] *Meditations*, 94.

as vivid and complex as my own. Aurelius reminded himself to look at people like a man, a woman, a human; to strip them down to their humanity under the masks, the fashion, the ethnicity, the profession, and to see them as a child just as I was a child. Everyone has a story.

One of my first jobs after my first tour of military duty was as a content writer for the Franklin Covey company, the time management experts and creators of the Day Planner. I remember a story from the *Seven Habits of Highly Effective People*, written by Stephen Covey. One of the seven habits was, "Seek First to Understand, then Be Understood." The story, as I remember it, was about the author riding a subway and observing two rowdy children running wildly and noisily about, bumping into people, and generally creating hate and discontent among fellow travelers. The father of the children did nothing to prevent it. When Mr. Covey approached the man and asked that he reign in his wild progeny, the man responded with a weak apology, as though he'd snapped out of a daze, and said something like, "We just left the hospital where their mother died. I don't know what to do."

We are not alone. If we pay attention, we realize that the vivid and complex lives of those around us are as saturated with at least as much pain as our own. When we recognize each other, when we *see* one another, even for a moment, the shared burden of life is lighter. It is through shared understanding that our lives are given context. Unless I first understand you in the context of your life, I have no other understanding to offer. Comprehending and feeling how we relate is a kind of rebirth into a shared life. As U.S.

Marines say when they toast each other, "I am never above you, never below you, always beside you." It's not *my* life, it's *ours*. You're not heavy, you're my brother and you're my sister. We are not meant to be alone.

Gratitude. "The best way to enjoy your job is to imagine yourself without one." – Oscar Wilde

Andrew Huberman discussed the major and long-lasting effects of a gratitude practice through a neurobiological lens. Huberman defines it as a "pro-social" behavior that improves interactions with ourselves and others, citing neural circuits in the brain specifically designed to respond to such behaviors versus those designed for defensive behaviors. He said that it can improve subjective well-being and improve resilience to trauma by both "reframing" previous trauma and "inoculating" against the effects of future trauma by "shifting how the fear and defense networks function in the brain."

An effective gratitude practice improves social connections and relationships and has an "outsized" positive effect across the spectrum of human experience. Huberman demonstrated that data shows the potency of an effective gratitude practice is on par with the benefits of intense physical exercise. The activation of pro-social circuitry not only improves experience but enables the extraction of a richer level of detail from an experience. A consistent practice of gratitude can shift our mental circuitry so that the pro-social circuitry dominates our mindset and results in higher levels of default happiness instead of a defense-dominated and generally negative outlook.

Huberman dives into the science of the medial prefrontal cortex, how it functions, and the positive effects that gratitude has on its operation. The medial prefrontal cortex, Huberman says, sets the *context* for everything in your life. Moreover, it is involved in the release of positive hormones like dopamine. The power of our attitude toward an experience activates the medial prefrontal cortex in a way that can physiologically alter the experience, making it either more positive or more negative. Huberman uses the example of taking an ice bath. The physical discomfort is "nonnegotiable", but the mental framework with which we view it determines how the medial prefrontal cortex responds to it, e.g., the difference between *choosing* to take an ice bath and *being forced* to take one. Though not fully understood, the medial prefrontal cortex can set the context for an experience, adjust "reflexive" neurocircuitry, and biologically increase positive health benefits.

Huberman points out that we cannot lie to ourselves. Glibly saying that "every experience is a learning experience" does not change the way our bodies react to the experience. The complexity and plasticity of neurocircuitry are such that it requires consistent practice over time to achieve lasting effects. Our brains know whether an experience is "good" for us regardless of bumper sticker mantras. We cannot activate the "positivity" network on the spot when confronted with life events but must shift the balance of the scales toward the positivity side through ongoing practice.

Huberman outlines ineffective and effective gratitude practices when the goal is neurological adaptation. Common myths pervade and ineffective practices are ubiquitous. One less effective example is a gratitude list where you recite or jot down a list of things for which you are grateful. A gratitude list is certainly not harmful, but scientific studies discount the effectiveness of the list technique in shaping neurocircuitry, except in cases of intentional autonomic arousal that can heighten the benefit somewhat. The most "potent form of gratitude practice" is not achieved when you *give* gratitude but when you *receive* it. Huberman cites a study where co-workers wrote gratitude letters to and about another and read them to them. The recipients' brain activity indicated a potent neurological response, far more than the outward-directed list approach.

The human brain is wired to respond to stories. Huberman cites a study where participants listened to stories of Holocaust survivors who were helped by others and survived. The listeners' neurocircuitry was powerfully affected as they began to identify or associate with the people in the stories, as they put themselves in the minds of the people. In terms of constructing an effective gratitude practice alone, without the participation of another person, is to seek stories that inspire based on the "beauty of the human spirit" or people's efforts to help another.

Consistency of practice is key. Instead of continually searching for meaningful stories, gratitude practitioners can intentionally recall instances in their lives when other people expressed gratitude *to them* for something that they said or did. Additionally, you can think deeply about the emotional experience of someone receiving help from someone else, even when you were not involved. What is necessary is that it moves you. Huberman suggests identifying a meaningful story and listing what the struggle was, how help was rendered, and how that "impacts you emotionally." This practice mimics many of the studies. When consistently practiced, weekly or several times per week for a minute or more, this positively triggers neurocircuitry and changes the ability of gratitude circuitry to activate. This happens relatively quickly, and you can experience increased feelings of well-being in short order. It's effective and it doesn't take long for benefits to kick in.

Intention matters. Huberman cited a study where they used magnetic resonance imaging to observe brain activity during exchanges between participants where a "benefactor" gave myriad sums of money to recipients either "wholeheartedly" or "reluctantly." The study showed that the intention of the giver more significantly affected positive brain activity in the recipient than did the sum of money. You can't lie to yourself about your true feelings. Your brain can't lie to your heart. Humans are wired to detect almost imperceptible tones and body language.

This power tends to be more acute in women than men. An evolutionist might point to survival and mate selection as the causative factors in the finely tuned development of such subtle detection abilities in women. Many of us experience this when something feels "off." Though we may be unable to articulate with precision that which does

He has been driven from Eden and knows he cannot return, but cannot grow beyond, or find redemption, so he languishes between nostalgia (the past) and anxiety (the future). Hamlet fails to bring to fruition either vision or practicality. He is strong enough to see but too weak to accomplish. "He is the prototype of so many modern men who see a noble world [or a noble vision of themselves] in their imaginations but don't have the means to accomplish it."[53]

Faust provides a model for a **Complex Man** who transitions to enlightenment through the integration of his shadow. The hinge period, as I describe it, between 3D and 4D consciousness is the "Dark Night of the Soul" captured in a Saint John of the Cross poem and subsequent treatise. Johnson elaborates, "This is the midlife crisis, the mute suffering of existential man . . . This is the experience of the intelligent man, the heroic man, the one who has reached the goal of modern consciousness . . . what happens when you reach the top of the ladder only to find that it was set up against the wrong wall. It is the very best man who suffers this Hamlet crisis."[54]

Johnson describes the Enlightened Man as a redeemed man, "gold-blooded", and whole. Referenced in a previous chapter, Johnson defines *happiness* as being in the happenings as they happen, or a version of that, and offers that being in what happens offers a bridge between the inner world and the objective fact of reality. The transition

---

53 Ibid., 47.

54 Ibid., 55.

fantasy," "unreal exercises of his imagination", he laments. Sancho switches roles with Quixote and admonishes him to continue the quest, but Quixote dies. "The true miracle of the story is the "sanchification" of Quixote and the "quixotification" of Sancho. The true journey of knighthood and chivalry has been to draw ego and shadow together, to diminish the split in personality indicated by the difference between the two. . . ."[51] Johnson then turns to Hamlet to represent the 3-dimensional man.

"In Hamlet we find the man of tragedy, he who makes chaos and failure of everything he touches . . . Hamlet is the most profound example in all of literature of the divided man." (Ibid, 35) Hamlet fails to synthesize paradox within himself, that of masculine/feminine, order/chaos, or self/shadow. He is indecisive and "pale-blooded." Vacillation is his undoing, a hallmark of the Complex Man. Hamlet teaches us that the price of indecision is much higher than a "wrong" decision. He knows too much to be simple but not enough to be whole. He is caught between vision and practicality, that familiar gap between the abstract and the tangible. Hamlet can imagine a better world but lacks the means to realize it. Caught up in words, he cannot act. Also, he patently rejects, even destroys, the feminine beauty and wisdom available, as represented by Ophelia and his mother. "All feminine elements whither in the face of three-dimensional consciousness."[52]

---

51 Ibid., 29.

52 Ibid., 43.

not ring true, we can often sense it. Gullibility in a person often points to an inability to detect cues and appreciate when he or she is being duped. A gratitude practice of any kind requires genuineness.

In summary, an effective gratitude practice must be grounded in a story. The story must depict instances of genuine altruism between humans, or a memory from your life where you received heartfelt thanks, though stories of animals helping animals can work. Capture a few of the most important bullets from the story to reference, including what the recipient felt like both before and following the gratitude. Devote 1-5 minutes of uninterrupted focus, three times per week or more, at a time of day that you can consistently devote to it. Your practice can include calming breathing or other focus rituals, but they are not necessary.[62]

Less is More. "We can choose between quality and quantity in all things."[63]

In an anthology titled *Less is More: A Collection of Ancient and Modern Voices Raised in Praise of Simplicity*, the author of the Forward, an economist, proposes two forms of logic: *straight-line* and *curved*. As in paradox, curved logic results in absurdities being possible, e.g., when a hindrance becomes a help or help becomes a hindrance, a militant pacifist, or less is more. He says,

---

[62] "The Best Gratitude Practices", YouTube, Huberman Labs Podcast, 2021.

[63] G. VandenBroek, *Less Is More: An Anthology of Ancient & Modern Voices Raised in Praise Of Simplicity* (New York: Inner Traditions, 1991), 22.

"Self-imposed limits, voluntary restraint, conscious limitations—these are life-giving and life-preserving forces. He goes on to describe a "New Economics", wherein progress, productivity, efficiency, and the "substitution of 'scientific method' for common sense" are only healthy "up to a point." Straight-line logic is indispensable to our relation to the material world but fails at the boundaries of spiritual substance.

Our *absolute* human needs are few enough that a moderate and moderated economic structure can meet them. He says, "There is no greater joy in life than the discovery of . . . *curved logic*. Less is more has the power of liberating you. The less you need, the less you need to worry; and the less worry there is, the better are likely to be your personal and suprapersonal relations . . . For what we need is so little that any system of good will [sic] can provide it. It follows that it is not so much a matter of "system" but of good will—and this depends on our own inner understanding."[64]

What you're looking *for* you're looking *with*. To search for God is to insult God. He's here, all around. Within the context of service to the Common Good, giving your full attention to each task at hand imbues routine activity with purposefulness. The *why* animates the *what*. To discover the mystical in the mundane cultivates contentment amidst circumstances, it synthesizes human wholeness, and it brings peace and order to the work-a-day chaos of our lives. The Holy Grail we seek is not so far from us, as

---

[64] *Less Is More*, xiii.

we may believe, though it remains hidden in plain sight. Whether we seek to be more functional in our current realm or to begin to understand reality through a non-material (i.e., spiritual) framework, we must eventually shift from a mindset of deprivation to one of abundance. I am not moving away from something but toward something else. Discipline involves resistance to and avoidance of old ways, but keep your eye on what you gain, not what you lose. An example is that "Therapy may release *from* addiction; spirituality releases *for* life."[65] Anything that I may "lose" along the way is replaced in ways too profound to speak.

Bruce Lee said that all mastery runs to simplicity. The only thing you've ever done well and the only thing you'll ever do completely is that which captivates you. It is in our nature to act with our whole hearts. When we give ourselves fully to those things we must do or choose to do, in their turn and time, and if they are of enduring value, we experience the "kingdom of the heavens at hand." The Great Spirit resides in everything. Experiencing it doesn't change anything in this world, but it changes everything in my life. So it is that I pass from deprivation to abundance, from desperation to inspiration, from chaos to contentment, from pain to peace, from hell to heaven, from fear to love, and from death to life.

"Don't waste the rest of your time here worrying about other people—unless it affects the common good. It will

---

keep you from doing anything useful."[66] External societal pressures often pale in comparison to the pressure we inflict on ourselves. It is tough enough out there. We are destined to scratch our living from the ground through toil and sweat, which is miserable enough without manufacturing additional internal misery to accompany it. So, take it easy. Don't worry about other people's opinions. Worry about yourself. Do your work and do your best. It's not anyone's job to decide where the chips fall. Remember that, all else being equal, the most relaxed boxer wins.

"To welcome with affection what is sent by fate. Not to stain or disturb the spirit within him with a mess of false beliefs. Instead, to preserve it faithfully, by calmly obeying God—saying nothing untrue, doing nothing unjust. And if the others don't acknowledge it—this life lived with simplicity, humility, cheerfulness—he doesn't resent them for it and isn't deterred from following the road where it leads: to the end of life. An end to be approached in purity, in serenity, in acceptance, in peaceful unity with what must be."[67]

---

[66] *Meditations*, 22.
[67] Ibid., 27.

Conclusion

I once received a special gift from fellow soldiers in my battalion. They printed on a framed canvas a picture of a Spartan soldier with Aurelius' words, *"Waste no more time arguing about what a good man should be. Be one."* I hung it on the wall across from my desk and pondered it daily.

What they could not have known was that I had begun to earnestly wrestle with the question, "What is a good man?" As I approached the end of my military career, I had grave doubts about myself. Or maybe they did know and sought to guide me toward the simplicity of the heart and away from the complexity my mind would make of that question. I have been nothing during my adulthood if not stubborn. I have insisted that I learn any lesson in the toughest way possible, repeatedly, and slowly.

Almost a decade later, I am convinced that what is good and what is required of us is easily recognizable. Debate is unnecessary because our hearts already know. In our best or worst moments, we can choose to see what is good in each other. I recognize it in you when you cannot see it. Like my fellow soldiers, you recognize it in me when I am blind to it. Do justly, be merciful, and walk humbly.

I've written letters to young men while they endured the challenge of military Basic Training or Boot Camp. I remind them that earning anything of value in life, or meeting a challenge, is never what we expect it to be; it is neither as difficult nor as easy as we expect. Challenges have a way of surprising us. You cannot predict what will be hard and what will be easy. Hence, we must prepare each day for what we do not know and what we cannot know. We must focus our attention and devote our energy to what we can control, or do something about, and think as little as possible about the things we cannot control, which is almost everything.

- Take the Long View. A year is 365 days, of which we can only live one day at a time. We will have easy days and tough days. At the end of each day, if I take stock, learn, and let it go, I'll stack up way more good days than bad. At the end of a year, I'll be in better shape than I was when I started it.

- During each day, engage the targets in front of you. Tomorrow's problems are exactly that. Do one thing at a time. Do it to the best of your ability until it's done. When it's done, it's done. Move on to the next best thing.

- Celebrate victories briefly and magnanimously. Celebrate failures in the same fashion. Drive on.

- Go to bed humble and grateful. Whatever your idea of God is, thank it for showing you some grace that day. At the very least, you survived. Turn the page. Sleep well.

- Wake up hungry. Pop out of bed like a piece of toast and bear hug a new day! You've been given another shot. Get moving, stick to your plan, and don't get your feelings hurt when it doesn't go your way and nobody seems to care.

- This is your life, no one else's. Adapt to what comes. Improvise as necessary. Hook and jab. Stride and glide. You won't always win, but you can always go down swinging. Getting knocked on your back puts you in a perfect position to look up at the stars.

We owe it to ourselves and each other to see what is good, to speak it, to do it, and to be it. We're built for it. Our finest natures reside within us, yearning to be freed.

"May the Father bless you and keep you, shine his face on you and be gracious to you, lift up his countenance on you and give you peace (Numbers 6:24-26)."

Bibliography
(*Further Reading*)

Adler, M. & Van Doren, C. (1972). *How to Read a Book.* Simon & Schuster.

Allen, D. (2015). *Gettings Things Done: the art of stress-free productivity.* Penguin Books.

Aurelius, Marus. (2022). In Daily Stoic Leatherbound Edition, *Meditations.* Modern Library, Penguin Random House LLC.

Barondes, S. (2012). *Making Sense of People: decoding the mysteries of personality.* Pearson Education, Inc. publishing as FT Press.

Buckingham, M. & Clifton, D. PhD (2001). *Now, Discover Your Strengths.* The Free Press.

Chamberlain, C. (1984). *A New Pair of Glasses.* New-Look Publishing Company.

Csikszentmihalyi, M. (1990). Paperback, *Flow.* HarperPerennial Modern Classics.

Duhigg, C. (2014). *The Power of Habit: why we do what we do in life and business.* Random House Trade Paperbacks.

Epictetus (2006). *The Discourses: Books 1-4.* Nu Vision Publications, LLC.

Gilbert, S. (1996). Etymologies of Humor: Reflections on the Humus Pile. http://sincronia.cucsh.udg.mx/etymolog.htm. Universidad de Guadalajara.

Henry, W. (1994). *In Defense of Elitism*. Anchor Books Division of Random House, Inc.

Johnson, Robert A. (1987). *Ecstasy: understanding the psychology of joy*. Harper and Row Publishing.

Johnson, Robert A. (1991). *Owning Your Own Shadow: understanding the dark side of the psyche*. HarperOne.

Johnson, Robert A. (1991). *Transformation: understanding the three levels of masculine consciousness*. HarperOne.

Junger, S. (2016). Paperback, *Tribe: on homecoming and belonging*. Harper Collins.

Kahn, D. *Krav Maga History*. www.israelikrav.com.

Kahneman, D. (2011). *Thinking, Fast and Slow*. Farrar, Straus and Giroux.

Koch, R. (1998). *The 80/20 Principle: the secret of achieving more with less*. Currency Doubleday.

Kurtz, E. and Ketcham, K. (1992). *The Spirituality of Imperfection: storytelling and the search for meaning*. Bantam Books.

Montaldo, J. (2004). *Dialogues with Silence: prayers and drawings*. Harper San Francisco.

Moon, G., (2018). *Becoming Dallas Willard: The Formation of a Philosopher, Teacher, and Christ Follower*, IVP Books (an Imprint of InterVarsity Press)

Scott, K. (2019). *Radical Candor: be a kick-ass boss without losing your humanity*. St. Martin's Press.

Sozhenitsyn, A. (1985). *The Gulag Archipelago: an experiment in literary investigation*. HarperPerennial Modern Classics.

Stockdale, J. (1995). *Thoughts of a Philosophical Fighter Pilot*. Hoover Institution Press.

Taleb, N.N. (2014). *Antigragile: things that gain from disorder*. Random House Trade Paperbacks.

Tiebout, H. (1999). *The Collected Writings*. Hazeldon Publishing.

Tsatsouline, Pavel. https://www.strongfirst.com/. *Enter the Kettlebell: strength secret of the soviet supermen, Kettlebell Simple and Sinister, The Naked Warrior: master the secrets of the super-strong using bodyweight exercises only, The Quick and the Dead: total training for the advanced minimalist, and Kettlebell AXE: high speed, low drag alternative to HIIT*. StrongFirst Publishing.

VandenBroek, G. (1991). *Less is More: an anthology of ancient & modern voices raised in praise of simplicity.* Inner Traditions International.

Willard, D. (1998). *The Divine Conspiracy: rediscovering our hidden life in God.* Harper San Fransico.

Willard, D. and Simpson, D. (2005). *Revolution of Character: Discovering Christ's pattern for spiritual transformation.* NavPress.

Willink, J. (2020). *The Code. The Evaluation. The Protocols. Striving to Become an Eminently Qualified Human.* Jocko Publishing.

Connect with Blacksmith Publishing

www.thepinelander.com

www.blacksmithpublishing.com